LEARNING FOR LIFE AND WORK
IN CLOSE-UP
YEAR 8

COLOURPOINT EDUCATIONAL

Paula McCullough

© Paula McCullough and Colourpoint Creative Ltd 2013

ISBN: 978 1 780730 26 4

First Edition
First Impression

Layout and design: April Sky Design, Newtownards
Printed by: GPS Colour Graphics Ltd, Belfast

All rights reserved. No part of this publication may be reproduced, stored in a retrieval system or transmitted in any form or by any means, electronic, mechanical, photocopying, scanning, recording or otherwise, without the prior written permission of the copyright owners and publisher of this book.

Copyright has been acknowledged to the best of our ability. If there are any inadvertent errors or omissions, we shall be happy to correct them in any future editions.

Pages 94 and 95 constitute an extension of this copyright page.

The Author

Paula McCullough has 25 years experience of teaching in Northern Ireland and examining at GCSE, AS and A2 level. She is currently head of the Religious Education Department at Methodist College Belfast and also teaches Learning for Life and Work.

Acknowledgements

Once again, it has been a pleasure to work with Rachel Irwin, Education Editor at Colourpoint. I would also like to thank Colourpoint Books for giving me the opportunity to work on this new series of books for KS3.

Thanks are also due to my family, husband Frazer and sons Peter and Michael, for putting up with me when I became totally engrossed in writing.

I would like to dedicate the series 'LLW in Close-Up' to Michael Spence. During his brief time as an Education Editor, Michael introduced me to writing for Colourpoint.

Thank you, Michael. Without you, my writing projects might never have happened.

COLOURPOINT EDUCATIONAL

Colourpoint Creative Limited
Colourpoint House
Jubilee Business Park
21 Jubilee Road
Newtownards
County Down
Northern Ireland
BT23 4YH

Tel: 028 9182 6339
Fax: 028 9182 1900
E-mail: info@colourpoint.co.uk
Web site: www.colourpointeducational.com

CONTENTS

PERSONAL DEVELOPMENT

SELF AWARENESS
This is me 10
My beliefs 12
Influences 14
Feeling good about myself 16
Managing my work 18

PERSONAL HEALTH
Health matters 20
How to be healthy 22
Growing and changing 24
Substance abuse 26
Staying safe 28
Know the risks 30

RELATIONSHIPS
My friends 32
Getting on with people 34
Difficult situations 36
Sorting out problems 38
Boyfriends and girlfriends 40

CITIZENSHIP

DIVERSITY AND INCLUSION
My identity 44
Family life 46
Attitudes to others 48

HUMAN RIGHTS AND SOCIAL RESPONSIBILITY
What are human rights? 50
Children's rights 52
Where rights are denied 54

EQUALITY AND SOCIAL JUSTICE
It's not fair! 56
Nowhere to call home 58
Focus on The British Red Cross 60
Focus on UNICEF 62

CONTENTS...

DEMOCRACY AND ACTIVE PARTICIPATION
What is a democracy? 64
Getting involved in school 66
Why do we need rules? 68
Taking action in your local area 70

EMPLOYABILITY

WORK IN THE LOCAL AND GLOBAL COMMUNITY
Work in Northern Ireland 74
Buying and selling worldwide 76
New technology 78
Health and safety 80

CAREER MANAGEMENT
What am I good at? 82
Thinking about my career 84
Investigating jobs 86

ENTERPRISE AND ENTREPRENEURSHIP
Are you an enterprising person? 88
Having a good idea 90
Going into business 92

INTRODUCTION TO THE SERIES

This series has been written to meet the requirements of the KS3 Northern Ireland Curriculum. Each of the three books covers all three areas of learning: Personal Development, Citizenship and Employability. There is a progression through Years 8, 9 and 10, with one book for each year group. There are 40 sections in each textbook, with each section containing ideas and activities for a week of LLW classes. There is plenty of choice to allow for differentiation and the interests of pupils.

The CD has been written alongside the text and follows exactly the content of each numbered lesson. The materials on this resource include a pupil worksheet for every lesson, photographs for projection and additional activities.

Learning for Life and Work is about a young person developing as an individual, relating to others, taking their place in society as an active citizen, and looking to the future and the world of work. For this reason each book starts with Personal Development, progresses to Citizenship and concludes with Employability. However, the sections can be taught in any order to suit the school curriculum.

OVERVIEW OF THE SERIES

YEAR 8 BOOK

PERSONAL DEVELOPMENT	CITIZENSHIP	EMPLOYABILITY
SELF AWARENESS 1. This is me 2. My beliefs 3. Influences 4. Feeling good about myself 5. Managing my work **PERSONAL HEALTH** 6. Health matters 7. How to be healthy 8. Growing and changing 9. Substance abuse 10. Staying safe 11. Know the risks **RELATIONSHIPS** 12. My friends 13. Getting on with people 14. Difficult situations 15. Sorting out problems 16. Boyfriends and girlfriends	**DIVERSITY AND INCLUSION** 1. My identity 2. Family life 3. Attitudes to others **HUMAN RIGHTS AND SOCIAL RESPONSIBILITY** 4. What are human rights? 5. Children's rights 6. Where rights are denied **EQUALITY AND SOCIAL JUSTICE** 7. It's not fair! 8. Nowhere to call home 9. Focus on The British Red Cross 10. Focus on UNICEF **DEMOCRACY AND ACTIVE PARTICIPATION** 11. What is a democracy? 12. Getting involved in school 13. Why do we need rules? 14. Taking action in your local area	**WORK IN THE LOCAL AND GLOBAL COMMUNITY** 1. Work in Northern Ireland 2. Buying and selling worldwide 3. New technology 4. Health and safety **CAREER MANAGEMENT** 5. What am I good at? 6. Thinking about my career 7. Investigating jobs **ENTERPRISE AND ENTREPRENEURSHIP** 8. Are you an enterprising person? 9. Having a good idea 10. Going into business

YEAR 9 BOOK

PERSONAL DEVELOPMENT	CITIZENSHIP	EMPLOYABILITY
SELF AWARENESS 1. Personal responsibility 2. Knowing right from wrong 3. Pressures and influences 4. Targets and goals 5. Coping with school **PERSONAL HEALTH** 6. Aspects of health 7. Body matters 8. Moods and emotions 9. Addiction 10. Illegal drugs 11. Coping in an emergency 12. Safe at all times? **RELATIONSHIPS** 13. Peer group problems 14. Difficulties in family life 15. Getting on with other people 16. Dating relationships	**DIVERSITY AND INCLUSION** 1. Customs and festivals 2. Belonging to a group 3. Dealing with conflict **HUMAN RIGHTS AND SOCIAL RESPONSIBILITY** 4. Human Rights 5. Focus on the UDHR 6. Where rights are denied **EQUALITY AND SOCIAL JUSTICE** 7. Equal rights 8. Living in poverty 9. Focus on Stand by Me 10. Focus on Tidy Northern Ireland **DEMOCRACY AND ACTIVE PARTICIPATION** 11. Living in a democracy 12. Young people and the law 13. Community action 14. Conservation matters	**WORK IN THE LOCAL AND GLOBAL COMMUNITY** 1. The global economy 2. Different jobs for different people 3. Environmental issues **CAREER MANAGEMENT** 4. Skills and achievements 5. Changing careers 6. What does an employer look for? 7. Career opportunities **ENTERPRISE AND ENTREPRENEURSHIP** 8. Skills for an 'Entrepreneur'? 9. Being your own boss 10. Celebrity entrepreneurs

YEAR 10 BOOK

PERSONAL DEVELOPMENT	CITIZENSHIP	EMPLOYABILITY
SELF AWARENESS 1. Beliefs and values 2. Coping with pressure 3. Personal strengths and weaknesses 4. Body image 5. Ambitions for life and work **PERSONAL HEALTH** 6. Health and the whole person 7. Influences on health – Exercise 8. Influences on health – Diet 9. The effects of substance abuse 10. Coping with adolescence 11. Looking after yourself **RELATIONSHIPS** 12. Healthy relationships 13. Challenging situations 14. Being assertive 15. Sexual relationships 16. Teenage parents	**DIVERSITY AND INCLUSION** 1. Personal identity 2. Community relations 3. Towards a peaceful community **HUMAN RIGHTS AND SOCIAL RESPONSIBILITY** 4. Human Rights 5. Where rights are denied – Child marriage 6. Where rights are denied – Torture **EQUALITY AND SOCIAL JUSTICE** 7. Social justice 8. Refugees 9. Focus on Education for All 10. Focus on Disability Action **DEMOCRACY AND ACTIVE PARTICIPATION** 11. Government in Northern Ireland 12. Crimes and punishments 13. Volunteering 14. Taking action	**WORK IN THE LOCAL AND GLOBAL COMMUNITY** 1. Challenges and changes 2. The local community 3. Rights and responsibilities at work **CAREER MANAGEMENT** 4. The next step 5. Options for employment 6. Essential skills 7. Careers advice **ENTERPRISE AND ENTREPRENEURSHIP** 8. Enterprise at work 9. Social enterprise 10. Small businesses in the community

SKILLS AND CAPABILITIES KEY

Icons are used in the text to show where an activity uses the cross-curricular skills, thinking skills and personal capabilities required by the Northern Ireland curriculum for KS3.

CROSS-CURRICULAR SKILLS

- **COM** Communication
- **ICT** Using ICT
- **MA** Using Mathematics

This icon is used to show that supporting activities and additional material are available on the CD ROM.

THINKING SKILLS AND PERSONAL CAPABILITIES

- **WO** Working with Others
- **MI** Managing Information
- **SM** Self-management
- **TPD** Thinking, Problem-solving, Decision-making
- **BC** Being Creative

PERSONAL DEVELOPMENT

**SELF AWARENESS
PERSONAL HEALTH
RELATIONSHIPS**

PERSONAL DEVELOPMENT

SELF AWARENESS
1. THIS IS ME

We are learning about:
- What it means to be unique
- Our different roles and identities
- How life experiences can shape us

YOU ARE UNIQUE
No one is exactly the same as another person. Your feelings, likes and dislikes, things you are good at and your experiences all combine to make you special. You will of course share things in common with other people, especially those you are close to. It is usual to see family members sharing some of the same characteristics. You and your best friend will probably enjoy taking part in the same activities, perhaps playing the same sport or sharing a similar taste in music. However, you are unique. No other person in the world is exactly the same as you or ever will be.

think about...

In what ways are you similar or different to your family and friends? Consider your appearance, your character and the things you like doing.

Do you agree that the world would be a very dull place if everyone was the same?

WHO AM I?
This is a difficult question and there can be many answers to it. You might act like a different person depending on the people you are with or the situation you find yourself in.

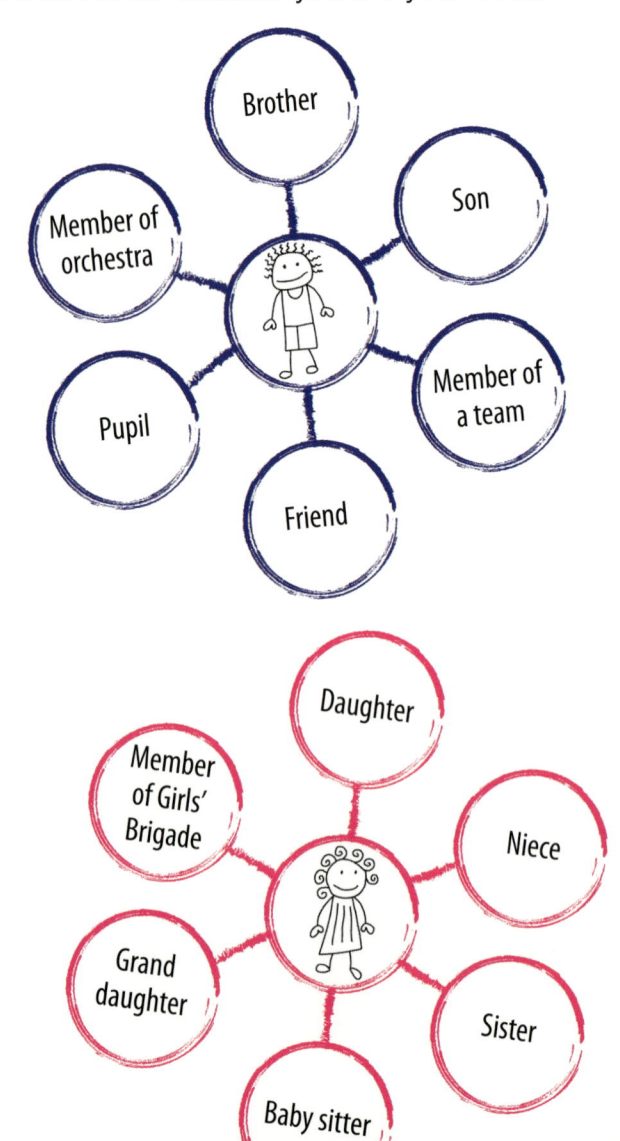

Roles: Brother, Son, Member of a team, Friend, Pupil, Member of orchestra

Roles: Daughter, Niece, Sister, Baby sitter, Grand daughter, Member of Girls' Brigade

activity...

Work in a pair. You have two minutes to tell your partner what makes you special, such as your character and what activities you enjoy doing. Your partner then does the same.

Join together with two or three other pairs to form a larger group. Each person tells the group three things about their original partner.

SELF AWARENESS

When you are on a sports team, it might be acceptable to shout loudly or run around, but not when you are a pupil sitting in a classroom with a very strict teacher! When you are with your family you probably behave differently than when you are with classmates your own age. You might find that you are more relaxed with close family members, such as a brother, sister or parent, than with relatives you do not see as often, perhaps grandparents or cousins.

You will also have different responsibilities according to which role you are in. Imagine you are helping to look after a younger brother or sister, or you are doing some jobs for a grandparent. Your responsibilities will be different than if you are going out with your friends.

MY LIFE STORY – SO FAR

If you look back over your life there will be some events that stand out in your memory. The things that were especially enjoyable, important or perhaps made your life change direction are what you may remember. Your life experiences are all part of what makes you a unique person. Some events in life are just there to enjoy, such as a birthday party or special holiday. Others can have a life-changing effect and can help to shape the person you are. These events might include moving house, changing school or coping with the loss of someone you love.

activity... BC MI TPD SM

Write your life story
Go as far back as you can remember (you might need a parent or relative to help with some very early details) and include the events in your life that you think are the most important.

You could illustrate your work with some photos of you when you were younger.

Draw a life map or make a timeline
This should also include the events in your life that you think are the most important. You could use photographs and drawings to illustrate your work.

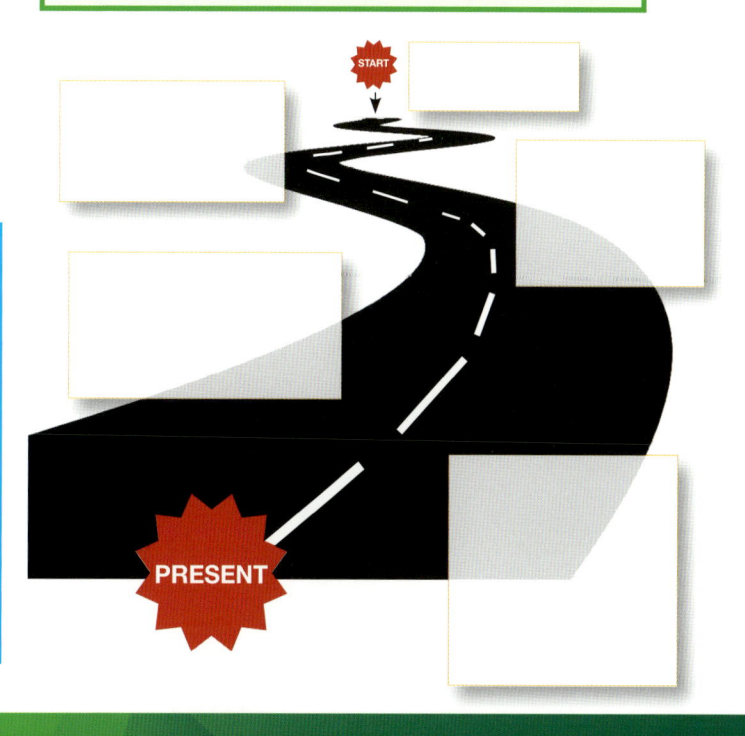

think about... TPD

What different roles do you have?

How do these different roles affect your responsibilities?

Are you still the same person even though you might behave differently with different people?

Which role do you like best or feel the most comfortable with?

START

PRESENT

PERSONAL DEVELOPMENT

2. MY BELIEFS

We are learning about:
- Where our beliefs come from
- How people show their beliefs
- Why beliefs are important

WHAT IS 'BELIEF'?

We all have beliefs of one sort or another. What we believe in shows something about the type of person we are, our personalities and our up-bringing. Our beliefs are another factor that helps to make each of us unique. But what is belief?

> **BELIEF**
> - An acceptance that a statement is true or that something exists.
> - A firmly held opinion or conviction.
>
> Source: Wikipedia, http://en.wikipedia.org/wiki/Belief

think about... What is your definition of 'belief'? How do your beliefs help to shape your character?

SM MI TPD

WHERE DO OUR BELIEFS COME FROM?

Everyone reading this will have shown belief in something today. You got out of bed believing a new day was about to start. If you travel by public transport, you would have waited for your bus and train believing it would arrive and take you to school. Did you stop to question whether your school would be open today and lessons would continue as normal? Sometimes we have beliefs because of **everyday experiences**.

Sometimes we have beliefs because of **facts and evidence**. Today, most people would believe that the earth is a spinning globe, as this is what scientists tell us. When you solve problems in maths, you probably show belief that the numbers and equations will always work out the way you expect them to.

$$\frac{1}{3} + \frac{3}{4} = \frac{3}{x+1} - \frac{4x}{x^2-1} \quad \frac{a}{x} + b =$$

Some beliefs depend on a person's idea of **right and wrong**. Most people would agree that it is wrong to steal, tell lies or to kill another person. Your ideas about the right or wrong way to act in a situation are known as your moral beliefs.

"I am a vegetarian. I don't eat meat as I believe it is wrong to kill animals for food."

"I believe it is important to care for the environment. I'm always on at my mum about recycling!"

"I believe that war and violence are always wrong. I would say I am a pacifist."

Your own **personal opinion** can also influence what you believe. Who do you believe is the most talented singer or the best sports team? You may well believe something totally different to your friend, but this does not mean that either of you are right or wrong.

SELF AWARENESS

Your **religion and cultural background** can have an important influence on what you believe. Being brought up to follow a religious faith, such as Christianity, Islam or Hinduism, for example, can shape your beliefs about what happens when we die or how other people should be treated.

"I believe I should pray five times a day. This is because I am a Muslim and follow what is written in the Qu'ran."

"I am an atheist. This means I don't believe God exists."

"My family are Hindu. We believe that when we die our souls will return to earth. This is called reincarnation."

"I believe men should not cut their hair or beards but allow them to grow. I am a Sikh and this is the teaching of my religion."

For discussion...
Do you share beliefs with other members of your family?
If so, what are they?
How do you (and your family) show your beliefs?

WHAT DO YOU BELIEVE?
Some people seem to have no problem making up their mind on certain issues. Perhaps their religion or up-bringing plays an important part in shaping their beliefs or maybe it is because they feel strongly about something. However, it's OK to be unsure about your beliefs or to keep an open mind. Sometimes you might even change your mind after listening to another person's point of view.

activity...

Look at the following statements. For each one, use the scale below to decide how strongly you agree or disagree:
- Strongly disagree
- Disagree
- Not sure/do not have an opinion
- Agree
- Strongly agree

I believe…
1. God exists
2. Science can explain everything about the world and our place in it
3. When I die I will go to heaven
4. No one should hurt or kill any human being
5. Everyone should give one tenth of their money to charity
6. It is important to make your best effort at everything you do
7. There are living creatures on other planets in our solar system
8. Ghosts are real
9. Animals should not be used for laboratory experiments
10. Science has all the answers

Compare your answers with the person beside you. Do you share any of the same beliefs? What are the main areas of disagreement?

Why is it important to respect what other people believe?

PERSONAL DEVELOPMENT

3. INFLUENCES

We are learning about:
- Who influences us
- Family influences
- The importance of friends

WHO INFLUENCES YOU?

Think back as far as you can. As you were growing up, a number of people were probably important in your life. Firstly, there may have been parents or carers, and possibly other close relatives such as grandparents. This group of people would have grown wider when you started school or playgroup. Can you remember your teacher from P1, or some of the first friends you made? All of these people you have come into contact with will have had an influence on you. As we grow up, we learn from other people. This is what helps to give us our values and a sense of what is right and wrong.

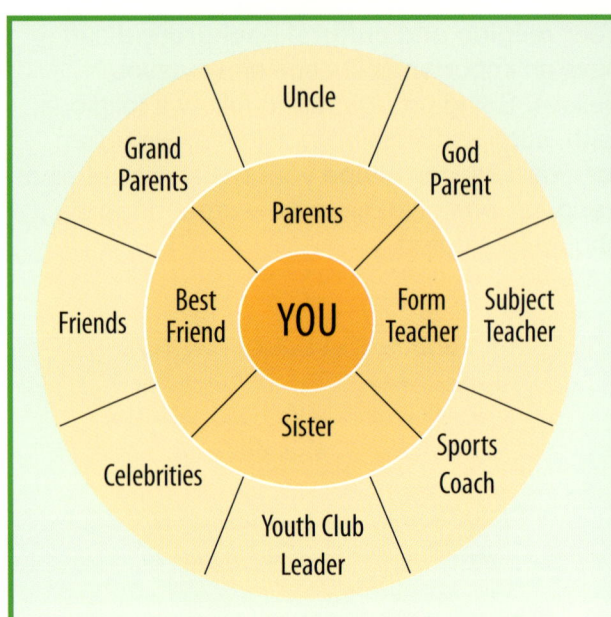

Look at your list of names. Beside each one, write down the reasons why this person influenced you. Here are some suggestions:

This person has an influence because he/she:

- knows me the best
- is concerned about me
- understands how I feel
- is responsible for me
- has time for me
- is someone I trust
- is older than me
- tells me what to do

activity...

Look at the diagram. It shows some of the people who may have had an influence in your life. The people in the inner circle may have influenced you more than the people in the outer circle.

Write down five people who you think influence you the most. Put them in order with the person who influences you most at the top.

For discussion...

What important decisions does a young person your age have to make in their life?

Whose opinion would influence you most when making these decisions?

How do your values influence your behaviour?

SELF AWARENESS

FAMILIES

Have you ever watched very young children playing together? You will probably notice that fights and tears can quickly develop if one child takes a toy another child is playing with. Humans do not automatically have an idea of right and wrong. The family home is where most children learn how to relate to other people and how to cope with life in the outside world. This is why close family members can have such an important influence on a young person's behaviour and values.

FRIENDSHIPS

Outside of our families, some of the most important influences will come from friends. We cannot choose our families, but usually we can choose who our friends will be. You will no doubt have made some new friends recently as you have started a new school. However, you probably still have friends from primary school, perhaps going as far back as P1. Friendships can be very important in life. As you have grown up, your friends will gradually have had more and more influence on values and behaviour.

Positive and negative influences

Not all influences from friends will be good ones. It is important to work out which influences are positive and which are negative. It can sometimes be helpful to take a friend's advice or go along with what your friends are doing. However, sometimes you will need to think for yourself and make your own mind up.

activity... MI TPD

Do you let your friends influence you, even when it might not be the right thing to do?

Read each of the situations below and answer YES or NO to the questions.

1. You are at the bus stop with a group of friends from your class at school. They start picking on someone who is not very popular. Do you join in with the bullying?

2. Two of your friends have had a row and fallen out. One friend says that if you do not take his/her side, they will never speak to you again. Do you take sides?

3. Your friend has volunteered to do some local voluntary work in the school holidays and wants you to join in. You are not sure if you can be bothered. Do you make the effort?

4. One of your friends is going to a party that your parents would never agree to. Your friend has suggested you should lie to your parents and pretend you are sleeping over at each other's houses. Do you agree to do this?

5. A close friend has expressed some opinions that you really do not like. Do you argue with your friend, even though they might not like to be challenged?

6. You have made a new friend, but none of your group likes this person. Do you drop your new friend?

PERSONAL DEVELOPMENT

4. FEELING GOOD ABOUT MYSELF

We are learning about:
- What is meant by self-image, self-esteem and self-confidence
- The importance of making friends
- The benefits of trying new activities

WHAT IS 'SELF-IMAGE'?

The word 'image' can mean a picture or an idea of something. 'Self-image' is therefore a picture or an idea that you have about yourself. Your self-image can include your appearance and what you think about your physical characteristics. It also includes how you rate your talents, abilities and achievements at school. People who are too boastful can be very unpopular, but it is not healthy to have a poor self-image. If you constantly think you look awful (when, in fact, you don't) or that you are a failure at everything (when you are really quite talented in some areas) this can make you unhappy and you will be unlikely to achieve your potential.

Self-confidence
This is your own opinion about your talents and abilities. If you think you can do things quite well, most of the time, then you would have high self-confidence. If you often lack confidence or feel nervous or unsure about doing something, then you would have low self-confidence.

Self-esteem
This refers to the feelings you have about yourself. If you are usually happy with who you are as a person, then you would have a healthy self-esteem. People with low self-esteem can find it difficult to accept praise for doing something well. They can be very critical about themselves and often think it is their fault when things go wrong.

think about...

How would you rate your self-confidence and self-esteem?

Give yourself a score, on a scale of 1–5, with 1 being the highest.

Do they change from day to day, depending on your mood or on what you are doing?

activity...

Make two lists: one of your good points and another of the things you are not so good at. Here is an example:

Things I'm good at
Making friends
Playing hockey
Art
Telling jokes

Things I'm not so good at
Keeping my room tidy
Maths
Being patient with my younger brother
Handing in homework on time

Try to keep your two lists roughly the same length. You should feel a sense of achievement looking at your list of good points. For the things you are not so good at, instead of thinking 'I'm just useless and there's no point trying', think of them as things you need to work on and write down three targets to help yourself to improve. Here is an example:

My targets
1. Ask my Maths teacher to explain what I don't understand.
2. Write down all my homework in my homework diary.
3. Spend half an hour each week tidying my room.

SELF AWARENESS

MAKING NEW FRIENDS

You have probably just started a new school. Maybe you have moved with a lot of your friends from primary school, or you might be the only one in your class from your old school. Either way, you will probably want to keep up with your previous friendships, but you will also need to make new friends. Making friends can be a great way to boost your self-confidence and self-esteem. If you realise that other people like you and enjoy your company, then can be easier to feel positive about yourself. If things get tough or you are feeling upset, then close friends can be a real help.

How do I make new friends?

Most people like to have friends who enjoy doing the same things they do. This does not mean that you have to be exactly like each other, just that you enjoy doing similar things. If you're really into sports, you probably will want friends who enjoy playing many of the same games you do. Think about your favourite things to do and try talking to your classmates at lunch or break about your hobbies. You're bound to find at least one person who's excited about the same things that excite and interest you.

TIPS FOR MAKING FRIENDS

1. *Remember to smile* – when you smile, people think you are friendly and easy to talk to. A grumpy frown can put people off.
2. *Say something nice* – If you give someone a compliment, it can be a good way to get talking.
3. *Ask questions* – You could ask someone where they live or who their favourite singer is. Asking questions does not mean you are being nosey, it shows you are interested in making friends.
4. *Make sure you have something to say* – If someone pays you a compliment or asks you something, don't just shrug and say OK, try to keep the conversation going.
5. *Be friendly to the people around you* – If you try to show an interest in the people around you, and are kind and friendly, then people will want to talk to you.

Some of the friends you make this year could remain your friends all the way through school and maybe even longer. It's worth the effort!

TRYING A NEW ACTIVITY

There are many opportunities and challenges now facing you in your new school. There will probably be subjects on your timetable that you did not study in primary school. There should also be the opportunity to try new sports and other activities. Perhaps you are finding some of your lessons a bit difficult to cope with at the moment. Taking part in an activity outside the classroom, that you enjoy and are good at, can be good for your self-esteem. It will also help you feel part of your new school.

activity...

Work in groups of about four for this activity

1. **Research** – You and your group have a week to find out as much as you can about clubs, societies and sports teams in your school. You could divide this up. For example, if one member of your group is already playing for a team, then this person could ask the sports teacher about other opportunities.
2. **Presentation** – Your group will record what you have found out as a leaflet, poster or PowerPoint.
3. **Sharing with the rest of the class** – You might be asked to show your PowerPoint presentation or display your poster for the rest of the class to see.

WO   MI   SM   BC   ICT

PERSONAL DEVELOPMENT

5. MANGING MY WORK

We are learning about:
- The challenges and opportunities of starting a new school
- The importance of being organised
- How to take responsibility for school work

A NEW SCHOOL

You have recently been through a big change in your life – moving school. Some people find changes in their life unsettling and unpleasant, as they like their everyday routine. However, change can also be exciting, giving you the chance to do something different and develop new skills. You should have plenty of opportunity for this now that you have moved on from primary school.

activity...

List the ways your school is different from your primary school. Beside each one note how you feel about this change and how you plan to cope with it.

Here is an example:

OLD SCHOOL
We stayed in the same classroom most of the time
NEW SCHOOL
We move around the school to lots of different rooms
MY FEELINGS
It's confusing – I am worried about getting lost
HOW I WILL COPE
I will have to be super-organised and make sure I know where I am going

Settling in

Perhaps you are finding the challenge of starting a new school a little bit daunting. There are plenty of things you can do to help you settle in more quickly. Here are some suggestions:

- **Learn your way around** – Don't add to the stress of starting a new school by getting lost and arriving late to class. Study a plan of the school and make sure you know where you are going.

- **Don't panic** – If something does go wrong, try to keep calm. If you have forgotten your dinner money or lost your school bag, find out who you go to for help.

- **Plan ahead** – Each evening, look at your timetable and pack everything you need in your bag. In the morning you could do a last minute check in case you have forgotten anything.

- **Check out the school rules** – There is no point in getting into trouble unnecessarily, so make sure you know what items are not allowed in school or which areas are out of bounds.

- **Talk to someone** – If something is bothering you, share your worries. Ask your Form Tutor who would be the best person to speak to, or talk to your parents or another adult you trust.

SELF AWARENESS

activity...

Work in a group of about four for this activity. You will need a large piece of paper or card and marker pens.

'Thought shower' how you have had to face up to changes in your life so far. For example, starting primary school or school, moving house, getting a new pet or falling out with a friend.

Take it in turns to give an example and write it down on your page.

Your finished page could be displayed or shown to others in the class.

GETTING ORGANISED

Your GCSEs and other school exams may seem like a very long way off right now, but your KS3 years are an important preparation. Getting into a good study routine now can help you to cope later on with the demands of schoolwork. It is also important to start taking responsibility for your own study. This means you are not just doing something because you have been told to do it. If your notes are in a bit of a mess, then organise your file without having to be told! Taking responsibility for yourself is an important step in growing up and being independent.

think about...

Ask yourself these questions, and be honest about how good your study habits are at the moment.

1. **Have I got a quiet place for homework?**
   You will need to have somewhere away from the TV and other members of the family so you can concentrate properly.

2. **Am I good at organising my work so I can meet deadlines?**
   It is important to plan what tasks you need to do and how much time should be spent on them.

3. **Do I keep a record of everything I have to do and the date the teacher expects it in?**
   It is difficult to meet deadlines if you have forgotten something. Don't rely on your memory, write everything down.

4. **Are my files and books in order?**
   It is important to keep on top of your class work. Are all your notebooks up to date? Do you always put your work in the right folder so you know where to find something?

5. **How good are my revision skills?**
   Revision skills will become more and more important as you progress through school, so get into good habits now. Do you just read your notes hoping you will remember something, or do you have techniques to help your learning?

If you think you are not too good in some areas, decide what you can do to make an improvement.

PERSONAL DEVELOPMENT

PERSONAL HEALTH
6. HEALTH MATTERS

We are learning about:
- What health is
- What it means to be healthy
- The different parts that make up a person

WHAT IS HEALTH?

We can use the word 'healthy' to describe many things. For example, you may have heard people talk about healthy relationships, healthy food and healthy finances. These do not seem to have anything to do with feeling fit and well.

What do we mean if we refer to a person as being healthy? Perhaps health is the opposite of being ill or in pain. But there is more to having good health than simply not having a disease or a medical problem.

HEALTH
- The state of being free from illness or injury.
- A person's mental or physical condition.

Source: www.dictionary.reference.com

think about... TPD MI

Is the above definition a good description of what it means to be healthy?

Do you think there is anything missing?

What else could you add to make the definition better?

WHAT DOES IT MEAN TO BE HEALTHY?

Think of your body as a machine. For it to function properly, all the parts have to be in good working order. If you are healthy, your body is working as it should. This could mean you are rarely absent from school with illnesses, you have a good appetite and plenty of energy for your daily activities. However, the human body is not a machine. Physical health is important but there is more to being healthy than feeling physically fit. Machines do not need to feel happy in order to work properly, but people do!

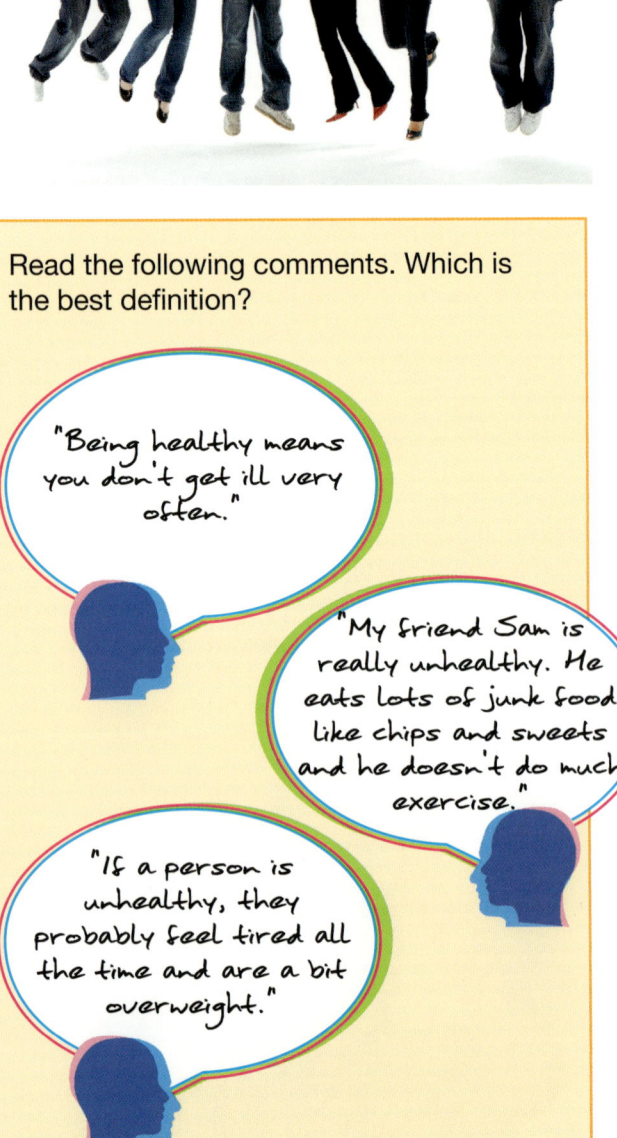

Read the following comments. Which is the best definition?

"Being healthy means you don't get ill very often."

"My friend Sam is really unhealthy. He eats lots of junk food like chips and sweets and he doesn't do much exercise."

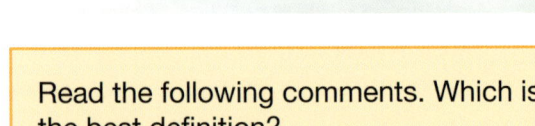

"If a person is unhealthy, they probably feel tired all the time and are a bit overweight."

PERSONAL HEALTH

"My dad is trying to be healthy. He cycles everywhere and eats lots of fruit and salad."

"Being healthy means you don't smoke, take drugs or drink too much."

All of these different parts are connected to each other, because they are all a part of you. If you do not look after your body by eating a poor diet or not getting enough sleep, then your mental ability may be affected and you will find it difficult to concentrate. If you are feeling angry or cross but do not handle these emotions properly, this could lead to unhealthy relationships with family of friends. If you want to be as healthy as possible, then everything has to be in balance.

activity... (MI)

What is your definition of 'health'? You could write your ideas on a sticky note and give it to your teacher to display on the board.

BEING A HEALTHY PERSON

Health involves the whole person. There are many different parts that make up a person and so being healthy involves all of these parts. You cannot ignore any of these areas if you want to be a complete and healthy person.

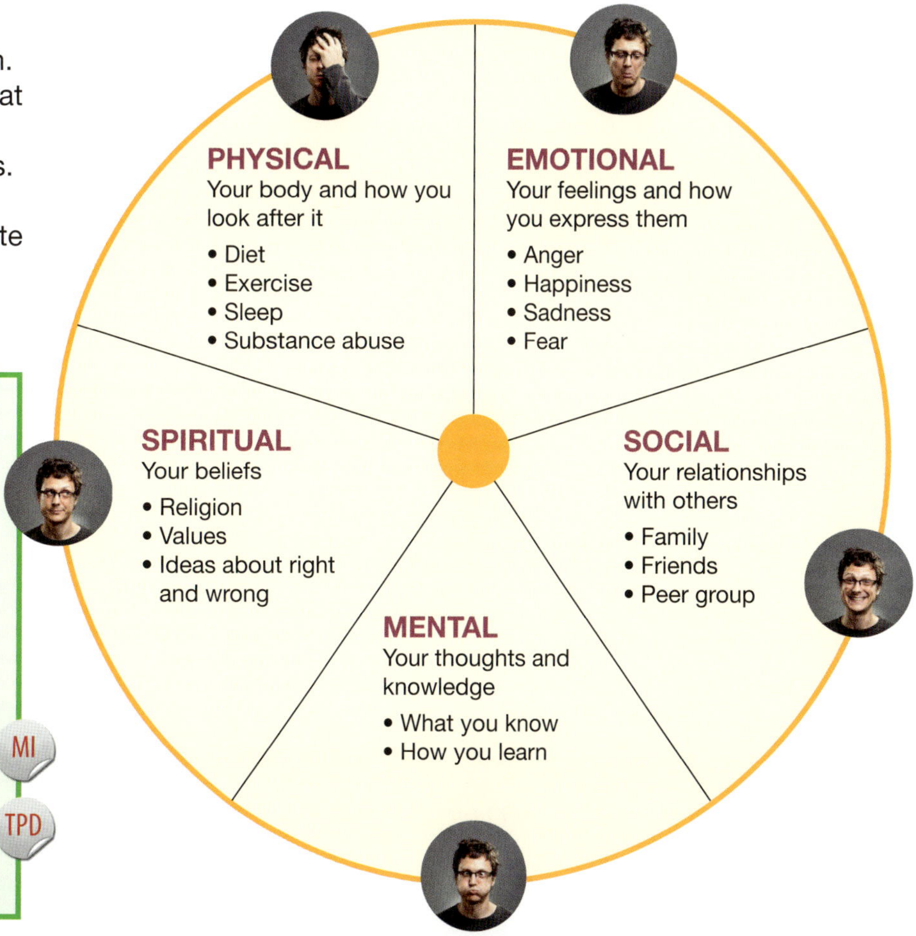

activity...

For each of the areas in the diagram opposite, write down two good points about yourself and one way that you could improve. For example, I get plenty of sleep and exercise but need to cut down on junk food. I get on really well with my dad and best friend, but I must try not to fight with my sister so much. (MI) (TPD)

PHYSICAL
Your body and how you look after it
- Diet
- Exercise
- Sleep
- Substance abuse

EMOTIONAL
Your feelings and how you express them
- Anger
- Happiness
- Sadness
- Fear

SPIRITUAL
Your beliefs
- Religion
- Values
- Ideas about right and wrong

SOCIAL
Your relationships with others
- Family
- Friends
- Peer group

MENTAL
Your thoughts and knowledge
- What you know
- How you learn

PERSONAL DEVELOPMENT

7. HOW TO BE HEALTHY

We are learning about:
- What it means to have a healthy, balanced diet
- The importance of regular exercise
- Personal hygiene

A HEALTHY DIET

At a time when your body is growing and changing a lot, it is important to look after it properly. One of the ways you can do this is to eat healthily. This does not mean going on a strict diet or giving up all your favourite foods. It simply means being aware of what you eat and making some healthier choices. Your body needs **protein** (to help you grow), **carbohydrates** (for energy), **vitamins and minerals** (to protect your body and help prevent illnesses) and **fibre** (to help your body get rid of waste). Which foods from the box below will give you these nutrients?

Getting the balance right
You need to eat a variety of different foods in your diet. These should include:
- Plenty of fruit and vegetables
- Plenty of starchy foods, such as bread, rice and pasta
- Some dairy products, such as cheese, milk and yoghurt
- Some protein foods, such as meat, fish, eggs and soya
- A small amount of food high in fat and sugar

---

activity... MA | MI | BC | TPD | ICT

Draw a large circle to represent a plate. Divide the plate into sections to show how much of each type of food you should eat each day. Illustrate each section of the plate with your own drawings of different foods. The following website might help you:
http://www.nidirect.gov.uk/the-eatwell-plate

Four steps to a healthier diet
1. Eat less junk food – Sweets, crisps and biscuits are usually high in sugar and fat but low in nutrients. They are called 'junk' because they supply empty calories.
2. Drink less junk – Try to cut down on fizzy drinks that are high in sugar. Drink water, milk or fresh fruit juice instead.
3. Eat more fruit and vegetables – 'Five a day' is recommended, but remember that this is the minimum amount.
4. Eat more fibre – This means more bread, pasta and rice. Go for whole grain or brown varieties if possible.

activity... MI | SM | TPD

There is a food diary on the CD for a 12 year old boy called Darren. List the good and bad points about his diet, and decide how you could make his eating choices healthier.

Try the quiz on the CD and see how much you know about keeping healthy.

MI | SM | ICT

KEEPING FIT

Eating a healthy, balanced diet will give you plenty of energy to enjoy an active lifestyle and get the right amount of exercise. Health experts recommend that young people get around one hour of exercise each day. About three times a week, you should exercise vigorously so you get out of breathe. It is also important to vary

PERSONAL HEALTH

the type of exercise you do. Some activities should be weight bearing to help build strong bones. This means you are on your feet rather than swimming or riding a bike. Exercise does not need to be boring – get together with some friends and take part in something fun!

Exercise is good for you
Here are some of the advantages of getting regular exercise:

- Exercise will help you to maintain the right weight for your height.
- You will look better and feel happier about your appearance.
- With regular exercise, you can avoid health problems when you are older, such as heart disease, type 2 diabetes, strokes and certain kinds of cancer.
- You will feel more relaxed as exercise relieves tension.
- Exercise can improve your concentration and help you do well at school.

activity…

Keep an exercise diary for a week. Note down each type of exercise you do each day, for how long, and how strenuous. Use the following rating:

1. **Very gentle exercise** – hardly out of breath
2. **Moderate exercise** – breathing heavier than usual
3. **Strenuous exercise** – breathing heavily and possibly sweating as well

OUTSIDE AS WELL AS INSIDE

It is important to look after your body on the outside as well as the inside. Keeping clean is good for you, especially during puberty when your skin and hair may be a bit greasier than usual. Remember:

- Always wash your hands after going to the toilet.
- Wash your hands before handling food and eating.
- Brush your teeth at least twice a day, morning and evening.
- Wash, shower or take a bath regularly to keep your skin clean.
- Always remove your make-up before getting into bed.

BEDTIME

Getting the right amount of sleep is another important part of being healthy. Sleep gives your body the chance to re-charge ready for the next day. A young person your age needs around 8–10 hours sleep each night. Do you often fall asleep listening to music or watching TV in your room? This is not a good idea as you do not get good quality rest if you fall asleep to background noise.

PERSONAL DEVELOPMENT

8. GROWING AND CHANGING

We are learning about:
- How our bodies change as we grow up
- What happens during puberty
- How to cope with these changes

GROWING UP
You have been growing and changing since you started life as an unborn baby inside your mother. During the first year of life you will have grown very fast. Now you are about to start another period of big changes as you go through puberty.

Everyone is different
There are no set rules for growing up. You may already be growing in all directions. On the other hand, you may be wondering if you will ever develop at all and stop looking like a child. Don't worry – by the time most people reach the end of their teens the differences have sorted themselves out.

All change
During puberty, you will not just change physically but in other ways as well. When you were younger, you probably spent a lot of time with your family. As you grow older, you will want greater independence and to spend more time with your friends. Your ideas about the opposite sex will also change. You may start to find them interesting, not boring or weird!

activity... MI SM BC WC
Collect pictures of yourself as a baby and younger child. If you cannot find photographs, ask someone who knows you well what you looked like and draw pictures of yourself. Make a personal album to show how you changed as you grew up.

think about... MI SM
You have recently started a new school. Think back to when you started school for the first time in P1. How have you changed since then? You will have grown taller and the shape of your body will have changed. Your hair might have changed colour and you will have a new set of teeth. As well as your appearance, consider your likes and dislikes, favourite things to do and who you were friendly with.

TAKING SHAPE
As you go through puberty, it might seem as if you are always growing out of your clothes. Your body will have periods of rapid growth, called growth spurts. You may find that you are putting on weight as well. This is your body's way of getting ready to make the change from child to adult. There will be different body changes for girls and boys.

Changes for girls
During puberty, girls start to develop a more curvy shape as their hips widen and breasts begin to develop. A girl will usually start her periods during this time. This shows that the parts of the body used for having babies are starting to develop. Girls will grow hair under their arms and around their genitals.

PERSONAL HEALTH

Changes for boys
A boy's body will become more muscular and his shoulders will become broader. Boy's voices 'crack' and will eventually become deeper. Boys get hairier too, also growing hair under their arms and around the genitals. The hair on a boy's chest and legs may get thicker and curlier. Eventually, he will grow hair on his face.

PUBERTY

What is puberty?
Puberty is the time when your body begins to develop and change, as you go from a child to an adult.

When does it happen?
It varies. For girls, puberty usually starts between the ages of 9 and 14 years. For boys it is often a little later, between 10 and 15 years old.

Why do these changes take place?
There is a small gland at the base of your brain, called the pituitary gland. It is only about the size of a peanut, but causes all these changes to take place. This gland releases special chemicals called hormones into your body. Depending on whether you are a girl or boy, the hormones go to work in different ways.

Does reaching puberty mean I am ready to have sex?
No. During puberty the parts of your body that will be needed in the future for making babies start to develop. It does not mean a young person is ready for a sexual relationship.

COPING WITH CHANGE
During puberty, your body starts to look different on the outside. Some young people can feel very anxious about the appearance of their body. Puberty hormones also change the way you feel on the inside. You might start to feel confused or have strong emotions that are new to you. Some young people become very sensitive or easily upset during puberty. Mood swings are also very common. Sometimes it can be very difficult trying to deal with all these new emotions. Try to remember that people are not usually trying to upset you or hurt your feelings on purpose.

I AM REALLY FED UP!

"I get aches and pains in all sorts of places."

"My face is so spotty, and my hair always seems greasy no matter how much time I spend in the shower."

"I am always hungry. My mum says I have turned into an eating machine."

"I never know how I am going to feel. I am happy one minute but really cross with someone the next."

"I feel sort of awkward and clumsy right now. I never used to feel like this."

"I always seem to get into rows with my dad. We just don't get on any more."

For discussion…
Have you shared these experiences?

Do you have any advice on how to cope?

PERSONAL DEVELOPMENT

9. SUBSTANCE ABUSE

We are learning about:
- What substance abuse is
- What addiction is
- The risks of smoking and drinking alcohol

WHAT IS SUBSTANCE ABUSE?

'Substance abuse' is misusing a substance which can alter a person's mood or behaviour. 'Misusing' means you are using the substance in a way that is harmful to your body or health. The substance can be illegal, or something that is legal but not used in the correct way.

Substance abuse can involve the following:
- Taking an illegal drug (for example, heroin, ecstasy or cannabis).
- Taking a drug that has not been prescribed for you by a doctor (for example, tranquillisers).
- Using something legal that is dangerous (for example, alcohol or tobacco).
- Using a solvent for the effect it has on your body, not the use it was made for (for example, glue, lighter fuel).

WHAT IS A DRUG?

A drug is a chemical which alters the way your mind and body works. Doctors prescribe drugs to patients who need pain relief, healing from an illness, or help in coping with everyday life. Drugs become dangerous when people take them for other reasons, such as having fun or showing off. This is misusing drugs and can be illegal. Many drugs themselves are illegal, as they have no medical benefits and are known to be very harmful.

WHAT IS ADDICTION?

One of the dangers with drugs is that they are addictive. This means that your body quickly becomes used to the effect they have and you need to keep taking them. With some drugs, a person may become addicted as they feel they cannot survive everyday life without them. The more dangerous drugs, such as heroin or cocaine, lead to your body becoming addicted as well as your mind. With these drugs, to stop taking them can mean you become very unwell and get physical symptoms such as sickness, headaches and muscle cramps.

> **activity...** TPD COM WO MI
>
> Work in a group of about four for this activity.
>
> On a large sheet of paper, draw a spider diagram to show the reasons why people take drugs. Your teacher may ask you to present your ideas to the rest of the class.

LEGAL DRUGS

Alcohol

For a large number of people, drinking alcoholic drinks is part of everyday life. Many people drink to be sociable, to relax or perhaps because there is something to celebrate. However, it is important to remember:

- The law says you have to be over 18 years of age to buy alcoholic drink.
- Drinking alcohol is illegal in many public places, such as parks or on the street.
- Alcohol is a highly addictive and dangerous drug.
- Alcohol is a chemical with many uses in science and industry, for example, as a cleaning product or as a fuel.
- Alcohol can seriously damage the liver, stomach and heart.

PERSONAL HEALTH

Smoking and your appearance
It is not just your health that suffers when you smoke. A regular smoker can have:
Smelly breath, hair and clothes
Stained fingers, nails and teeth
Damaged skin, especially to the face as it is constantly in a cloud of poisonous fumes.

Alcohol and young people
There are health risks with alcohol at any age, but young people are especially at risk. This is because your body is likely to be smaller than an adult's and is still growing. Alcohol can reduce brain development in young people and there is more chance of damaging your liver if you drink regularly when you are young. For many young people, having too much to drink can lead to risky behaviour. This may include getting involved in crime, fighting or vandalism.

WHAT DO YOU KNOW ABOUT SUBSTANCE ABUSE?
Friends might tell you things about addictive substances that are untrue. It is important to know the facts. Try the quiz on the CD to see how well informed you are about smoking, alcohol and drugs.

Smoking
Tobacco is a legal drug, but you have to be 18 years of age to buy cigarettes and smoking is now banned in all public places. Health experts say that there is no safe level of smoking as every cigarette causes harm to your body – or to someone else's! The advice to anyone who does not smoke is not to start. Here are some facts about smoking:

- The drug contained in tobacco is called nicotine and it is highly addictive. Many people want to give up smoking but cannot manage to do it.
- Smoking is very damaging to health and can cause cancer of the mouth, throat and lungs. It can also lead to heart disease.
- The younger a person is when they start smoking, the more likely they are to die early.

activity...

ROLE PLAY
Work in groups of about four for this activity.

Choose one of the following situations to role play in your group:

- You are on a school residential trip. Four of you are sharing a room. One night, you are eating crisps and drinking coke in your room before you go to sleep. One friend produces a small bottle of vodka to put in the coke. How do the rest of you react?

- You need to borrow a pencil to do your homework. You look in your 14 year old brother or sister's school bag and discover a pack of cigarettes. Role play the scene where you confront your brother or sister, then tell your parents.

27

PERSONAL DEVELOPMENT

10. STAYING SAFE

We are learning about:
- Safety for pedestrians and cyclists
- How to cope in an emergency
- Health and safety in school

ROAD SAFETY

Our roads are getting busier. Every year, thousands of children and young people are hurt in traffic accidents. Whether you live in a city, town or rural area, you need to have road sense and be able to keep yourself safe.

BE SMART AND STAY SAFE ON THE ROADS

The Highway Code contains rules for all road users. These points are a summary of some of the advice for pedestrians:

- Always use the footpath, if there is one.
- If there is no footpath, walk on the right hand side of the road, facing the traffic as it comes towards you.
- When it is dark, always wear something bright, reflective or fluorescent.
- When crossing the road, always use a zebra or pelican crossing, if there is one.
- Make sure you know the Green Cross Code and always use it when crossing the road.
- Take special care when walking across bus and cycle lanes, or between parked vehicles.
- Do not wear your ear phones or listen to music when crossing the road, as you won't be able to hear traffic approaching.

ARE YOU A SAFE CYCLIST OR A RISKY RIDER?

There is more risk of a cyclist having an accident than any other road user, except motorcyclists. Statistics also show that the most dangerous age for cyclists is between 12 and 14 years. If you ride a bike, make sure you keep safe by following these tips:

DOs	DON'Ts
• Attend a Safer Cycling training course. You will learn how to ride correctly and how to handle traffic.	• Carry bags on the handle bars. Use a ruck sack on your back or have a special carrier on the back of your bike.
• Always wear a cycle helmet.	• Wear loose clothing that could get caught in the chain.
• If you cycle at night, have lights on your bike and wear something reflective or fluorescent.	• Ignore repairs to your bike. You need to keep it in good working order.
• Remember to give hand signals when turning left or right, so motorists know where you intend to go.	• Expect motorists to notice you.
• Take special care at roundabouts or when turning right.	• Take your hands off the handle bars (unless you are giving a hand signal) or your feet off the pedals.

IN AN EMERGENCY WHERE HEALTH OR SAFETY ARE AT RISK ...

1. Keep yourself safe
2. Get help
3. Help others only if you can do so without putting yourself in danger

PERSONAL HEALTH

SAFETY AT HOME

Many people think of home as being a safe place. However, it is worth remembering that most minor accidents happen at home. It is sensible to be aware of possible dangers to keep yourself and other family members safe. It is also smart to know what to do in an emergency. This can prevent a small accident from becoming more serious and may even help to save a life.

activity… COM WO MI TPD

Could you cope?
What action would you take in each of the following situations? Work in small groups and discuss what you should do.

1. You go to visit your grandad, who lives on his own. There is no answer when you knock on the door. You let yourself into the house and see him lying on the floor. What should you do?

2. You see a crash involving two cars. The people inside both cars seem to be hurt or in shock. You need to make a 999 call. How do you do this and what would you say?

3. It is hot and sunny. Your friend has been lying outside for hours, trying to get a tan. He seems to be getting badly burnt. What do you do to help your friend?

4. You are looking after a younger child and she scalds her hand in an accident with a hot drink. What do you do?

5. Your mum has cut her hand quite badly while cutting up vegetables. She has put her hand under the cold tap, but the bleeding won't stop. She calls to you for help. What do you do?

6. You and some friends are in the local park. You notice some syringes and needles lying on the ground. There are some very young children playing nearby. How do you keep yourselves and the young children safe?

HEALTH AND SAFETY AT SCHOOL

You might think that some of the rules in your school are silly or unnecessary. However, many of the rules will be there for health and safety reasons. When a large number of people are in the same building, such as a school or workplace, it is important to cut down the risk of accidents, especially when tools or apparatus are being used.

MI SM WO

For discussion…
What rules does your school have to keep pupils safe? Discuss each situation in pairs.

- Using tools in Technology
- Experiments in Science lessons
- Playing outdoor sports
- Using apparatus in PE
- Moving along the corridors
- Outside at break
- Cooking in HE
- Waiting for school buses

Do you know what areas are 'out of bounds' to pupils? What is the reason why you are not allowed in these areas?

activity… ICT COM WO MI BC

Work in pairs for this activity.

Make a short PowerPoint presentation giving health and safety advice for your school. Your presentation should be aimed at new pupils starting in Year 8.

PERSONAL DEVELOPMENT

11. KNOW THE RISKS

We are learning about:
- How to be responsible for your own safety
- What to do if you feel threatened when you are out
- Using the Internet safely

STRANGER DANGER

As you grow older and gain more independence, it is important for you to be able to look after yourself. We all have a right to feel safe when we are out and to walk through the streets without feeling frightened. Unfortunately, this is not always possible, so you need to be smart and make sensible choices. This does not mean being too afraid to go out and enjoy yourself. It is worth remembering that crimes against young people by strangers are very rare.

Staying safe when out and about
Your parents and carers have probably given you their own advice, depending on where you live. Here are some common sense tips to bear in mind as well:

- Stick to busy, well lit streets and avoid lonely paths and alley ways.
- Keep your mobile with you, but make sure it is out of sight.
- Try to avoid talking to strangers. If someone is bothering you and keeps trying to talk, give a brief, cold answer and walk away.
- If you think someone is following you, go to a place where there are people around, like a bus stop or shop.
- Make sure that lifts are arranged in advance and never accept a lift with a stranger.
- Avoid deserted public toilets. Go with a friend.
- If you are travelling alone on public transport, especially at night, try to sit with a family. If this is not possible, sit at the front of the bus near the driver.
- If you have to get off the bus at a lonely stop, arrange for someone to meet you.
- If you feel threatened, be prepared to shout loudly and attract attention.

activity...

What would you do?
What would be the best way to stay safe? Work in small groups and discuss each situation.

1. You are travelling home on the bus late at night. A stranger gets on and sits beside you, even though there are plenty of seats, and keeps talking to you. You have tried turning away but this has not worked.
2. You and a friend are walking home. It is starting to get dark and you are worried about getting into trouble at home for being late. Your friend suggests a short cut along a lonely lane that will save you 30 minutes.
3. You are in the cinema with some friends, sitting at the end of your group next to a stranger. During the film this person makes you feel uncomfortable by leaning over you too much and 'accidentally' brushing against you.
4. You usually walk home after youth club, as it is not very far. One night it is raining very heavily. There is a new

PERSONAL HEALTH

leader at the youth club who you have never seen before. He offers you a lift in his car.

5. You arrange to meet your friend at a fast food restaurant, but your friend is late. While you are waiting, a stranger asks if you would like to sit at his table and offers to buy you a cola.

COM WO TPD MI

Internet nasties

There are some nasty things on the net. Here are some examples:

- Cyber bullying
- Viruses
- Chain emails
- Seeing things you wish you hadn't
- Talking to 'weirdos'
- Someone using your photo in a way that upsets you

Can you think of any others?

BC MI

SAFE USE OF THE INTERNET

Using the Internet can be fun. You can stay in touch with your friends and have access to games, films and music. It is also educational and a great help with homework projects. However, it is sensible to be aware of the possible dangers of Internet use. Chat rooms can seem harmless, but talking to people you cannot see and do not know can be risky. People tell lies about themselves. Someone might say something that upsets or annoys you. If you like chatting online, then talk to family members or friends from the real world.

You might also like to post photos and information about yourself on social networking sites. However, you need to think carefully about what you are making available for everyone to see.

Important to remember

- 🙂 If you see anything online that upsets or worries you, always tell a parent or carer.
- 🙂 Always check before downloading or installing anything that it is OK to do so – otherwise you might get a nasty virus!
- 🙂 Agree rules with a parent or carer for your use of the Internet. Show them the sites you like to use.

- ☹ Never give out personal information to people that you chat to online. This includes your address, phone number and age.
- ☹ Do not send anyone a photograph, unless a parent or carer says it's OK.
- ☹ Not everyone in a chat room tells the truth about themselves. Sometimes adults pretend to be children and try to make friends with young people. Never arrange to meet someone you only know online.

FINALLY – Remember how to behave towards other people when you are online. Never use your computer or phone to hurt or annoy someone else.

activity... ICT COM BC MI SM

Design a poster suitable for a P5 classroom. The aim of your poster is to give advice to younger people about safe use of the Internet.

31

PERSONAL DEVELOPMENT

RELATIONSHIPS
12. MY FRIENDS

We are learning about:
- Why friends are important
- What makes a good friend
- How to cope with arguments

FRIENDS ARE IMPORTANT

An important part of life is having people to share things with, to talk to and to support you when things are not going well. Friends make you feel wanted, care about you and can play a big part in helping you to feel happy and healthy. Friendships can be especially important for young people. You may sometimes feel that family members do not understand your problems, but a close friend your own age can relate to what you are going through. Gaining independence is an important part of growing up and friendships can help with this. When you were younger, you probably spent most of your time with your family. Now you are growing up, you probably want to spend more time with your friends.

think about...

In what ways are your friends important to you?

What is a friend?
Look at the following statements about friends and decide if you:

a) agree
b) sometimes agree or
c) disagree

1. A friend should like doing the same things as me.
2. A friend must always be there for me.
3. A friend is someone my parents approve of.
4. A friend should cover up for me if I am in trouble.
5. A friend will never gossip about me to others.
6. A friend should share my beliefs and values.
7. A friend always says good things about me.
8. A friend is someone I can rely on.

Discuss your answers with the person sitting beside you.

WO TPD MI

REAL FRIENDS

Some of the friendships you make will be more important in your life than others. You might make friends with someone because you get the same bus or have to sit next to each other in class. You might drift away from this person if your routine changes and you no longer see them on a regular basis. You will probably go through life making many casual friendships. However, the really good friendships are the ones that will last, perhaps for your whole lifetime.

You feel good about yourself when you are with a good friend

"There are no rules about what makes a good friend – they could be a girl or boy, and they do not have to be the same age as you. It's the person that counts."

RELATIONSHIPS

"Good friends listen to you without passing judgement."

"It's great to know that someone relies on you, likes your company and takes an interest in your life."

"Good friends accept you the way you are. They do not try to change you."

People who are not good friends

Nobody is perfect and friends can sometimes be unkind or let you down without meaning to. However, if someone regularly acts in any of the following ways, they are not a true friend:

- Makes fun or you
- Talks about you behind your back
- Makes you feel bad about yourself
- Pressures you to do things you are not happy with
- Does not like you having other friends
- Bosses you about and makes all the decisions

People who behave like this towards you can lead to you having low self-esteem. It is better to spend your time with people who genuinely care about you and want to be your friend.

Remember to be a good friend

If you want to have good friends, it is important to be a good friend yourself. If your friend has a problem or needs support, then think about what you would want. A sign of a good, healthy friendship is that a friend will turn to you when things are difficult for them. This could be because your friend is unhappy at home or is in trouble at school. Do not tell your friend what to do and try not to act as if you have all the answers. However, be prepared to listen and give them space to make their own decisions. You can also be a good friend by respecting their privacy and not gossiping to the rest of your class about what may have been said to you in confidence.

activity... MA MI SM

Are you a good friend? Answer the quiz on the CD honestly to find out.

ARGUMENTS WITH FRIENDS

Sometimes we just don't agree with our friends. No matter how much you may try to avoid an argument, there can be a disagreement with someone close to you. This does not mean it has to be the end of the friendship. Sometimes working through a disagreement can make the relationship stronger and you will have a better understanding of each other. Arguments can take place for many reasons. Sometimes we have different ideas about what is right or wrong than our friends. We can also misunderstand people, or they can misunderstand us. A strong friendship will be able to cope with arguments and misunderstandings.

If you have an argument with a friend, remember these tips:

1. Do not be afraid to back down and apologise.
2. Always listen carefully to what your friend has to say.
3. Never say hurtful things you may later regret.

think about...

When did you last have a disagreement with a friend?

How could the argument have been avoided?

TPD

PERSONAL DEVELOPMENT

13. GETTING ON WITH PEOPLE

We are learning about:
- Why we need to relate to others
- What makes a healthy relationship?
- Healthy relationships with family and friends

WHY ARE RELATIONSHIPS IMPORTANT?

Think of all the people you come into contact with during a typical day. With some of these people, you will only exchange a word or two. With others you will spend a lot of time as they play an important part in your life. No matter how much time you spend with someone, it is important to get on with them. Meeting other people is all part of daily life.

Jordan sat down to breakfast and exchanged a couple of words with his brother. He was still half asleep. Then his mum reminded him about his dentist appointment later that day. At the bus stop, he chatted with some other boys from his class. When he arrived at school, Jordan had a few minutes to talk to his best friend then a teacher shouted at him to hurry up to registration…

think about… Why is it important to get on with the people we meet? How do you think you would feel by the end of the day if every contact with another person had led to a disagreement?

Having close relationships with people who are really special can help you to be happy and healthy. Knowing people care about you can be a great boost to your self-esteem. As a young person, you will have many different relationships with lots of different people, for example, members of your family, friends at school, people you see at youth club or play sport with. These relationships can be an important part of growing up and learning about the kind of person you are. Learning to get on with people when you are young can help you build long-lasting relationships when you are older.

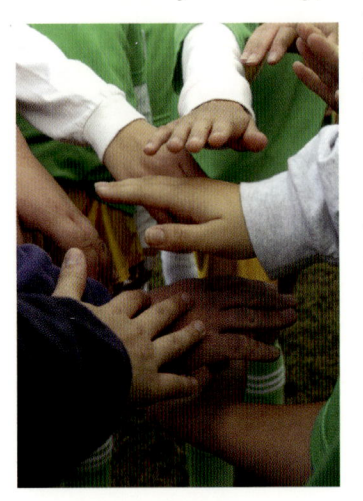

WHAT IS A HEALTHY RELATIONSHIP?

A healthy relationship makes you feel good about yourself. You enjoy being in someone's company and you feel safe with them, knowing they can be trusted and that they want what is best for you.

How can you build healthy relationships?

1. **It takes time** – Building a healthy relationship takes time, energy and care. Sometimes it will not be easy. You might get cross with someone or feel let down, but you know the relationship is worth it so you make an effort to sort out any disagreements. Healthy relationships don't just happen by accident.

2. **Talk and listen** – If you listen to someone, you show that you are interested in them and value what they have to say. When you share your thoughts and feelings with another person, you are showing that they are an important part of your life. In a healthy relationship, people are honest with each other.

3. **Spend time together** – A sign of a healthy relationship is that you like to be with someone and enjoy their company. This

could be because you like doing the same things, or perhaps your friend has a sense of fun and makes you laugh. In a healthy relationship, you know you can share your feelings with someone if you are feeling worried or upset.

4. **An equal partnership** – In a healthy friendship, there will be an equal amount of give and take. One person should not make all the decisions or boss their friend around. In a healthy relationship, the opinions of both people should be of equal value and both need to make an effort to make the relationship work.

NEWS ITEM
What makes you happy with life?
A big children's charity has asked 30,000 children what makes them happy - and unhappy.

Topping the list of unhappiness is 'not getting on with my family', but moving house and money problems also make children feel sad. The Children's Society reckons half a million children in the UK could be unhappy. But experts at the charity say they've also worked out what will make kids happy. Some of them are things that adults might have more control over.

The charity's six ways to be sure of growing up happy are:

- The chance to learn
- A positive view of yourself
- Important experiences
- Positive relationships with family and friends
- A safe home life
- Positive activities

Source: 'Chat: what makes you happy with life?', BBC Newsround, http://www.bbc.co.uk/newsround/16524141

For discussion…
What makes you happy with life? How important do you think good relationships are in making you happy? Use the priority pyramid on the CD to record your views.

QUALITIES OF A HEALTHY RELATIONSHIP
Think of the relationships you have that are really good. What is it that makes them special? Are there any of the following qualities in these relationships? Can you think of any others?

FORGIVENESS "If I mess up and let my friend down, it's important to know she'll forgive me."

SHARING "Friends should share with each other – their time, their things and their feelings."

RESPECT "We don't always agree but we respect each other's opinions."

HONESTY "My friend is always honest with me – even if it means telling me that my new hairstyle looks weird."

TRUST "I can trust my friend not to gossip about me or share my secrets with the rest of the class."

PERSONAL DEVELOPMENT

14. DIFFICULT SITUATIONS

We are learning about:
- Family relationships
- Coping with brothers and sisters
- Getting on with parents

HAPPY FAMILIES?

Building good relationships is an important part of family life. Your family is where you learn how to relate to others and cope with life in the outside world. You can usually choose who you want to be friends with, but you cannot choose your family! This is why family relationships sometimes need a special effort to make them healthy and strong.

Family relationships can be really good…
- You can relax and be yourself when you are with your family.
- It can be fun to enjoy things together, such as family celebrations or holidays.
- You might like doing the same activities as other members of your family.

Sometimes family relationships can be difficult…
- Your family know you really well, so they know how to tease you and wind you up.
- Family members can often be blunt and outspoken when pointing out your faults.
- If you have fallen out with a member of your family you cannot just walk away as you have to live with that person.

BROTHERS AND SISTERS

Sometimes it can take an extra special effort to build healthy relationships with brothers and sisters – especially if they are very annoying! There can often be feelings of jealousy between children growing up in the same family. Sometimes you might think you are being treated unfairly or that your brother or sister is the favourite one. **Sibling rivalry** is where the children in the family compare themselves to each other and compete for their parents' attention. This can lead to fights and name-calling.

activity…

Look at the following situations. Have you ever faced a similar problem? What advice would you give to each person?

CLAIRE'S PROBLEM
"I think it's so unfair the way my older sister gets her own way all the time. Just because she is studying for her GCSEs mum lets her off all the chores and I have to do extra. She also gets far more pocket money than I do, which is hardly fair as she does nothing around the house."

AHMED'S PROBLEM
"My little brother is so annoying. He's always going into my room and messes up my things. If I complain dad says I have to be more patient with him. He's spoilt rotten because he's the youngest and it's just not fair."

KEVIN'S PROBLEM
"I am not any good at most of my subjects in school. I like art and playing football. I get nagged a lot at home to study harder so I can be more like my older brother and sister. They are both really smart. I think my parents are disappointed with me."

RELATIONSHIPS

How to cope with brothers and sisters

Squabbles between children in a family are bound to happen and are all part of growing up. However, sometimes you need to make sure an argument does not get out of hand.

Here are some suggestions:

1. **Talk to your brother or sister** – Let them know that there is a problem and that you both need to work at sorting it out.
2. **Talk to your parents** – Let your parents know you are unhappy, especially if you think they are showing favouritism. Be careful how you go about this, so it does not look like you are just moaning.
3. **Be honest with yourself** – Are you really so hard-done by? Maybe *you* were spoilt a bit when *you* were younger, or perhaps *you* will get more freedom when *you* become a teenager.
4. **Try to understand** – If there has been a disagreement, ask your brother or sister to give their side of the story. Perhaps they are not totally in the wrong after all. If so, be prepared to apologise. This can be a great way to clear the air!
5. **Do something together** – Sharing an activity together could help you become closer. You might still annoy each other, but at least you could try and focus on what you have in common rather than your differences.

activity... (BC ICT MI)

Design a poster 'Top tips for coping with your brother or sister'. You could use a computer for this activity.

PROBLEMS WITH PARENTS

Here are two very common complaints for young people to have about their parents:

"They don't give me enough privacy!"

"I need more independence!"

Have you ever felt this way? Perhaps your parents like to keep a check on your Internet use, when you feel you could be trusted to monitor the sites you use for yourself. If you go out with friends, do you always have to say who you will be with and where you are going? You probably think the time when you have to be back is far too early. These issues can often lead to family arguments.

Young people need to have more independence as they get older. However, your parents or carers are probably not trying to spoil your fun or treat you like a baby – they are just trying to keep you safe. Perhaps talking to your parents about some new rules and trying to reach a compromise would help. Remember, though, that you will need to convince them that you are ready for more independence and greater responsibility. How do you think you could do this?

activity...

ROLE PLAY

Work in groups of two for this activity.

Choose one of the issues given above and role play an argument about it between a parent and a child. Produce two versions of the role play:

1. The young person is cheeky and the argument develops into a row.
2. The disagreement is settled as the young person stays calm and an agreement is reached.

(WO BC TPD)

PERSONAL DEVELOPMENT

15. SORTING OUT PROBLEMS

We are learning about:
- How to show feelings
- Coping with conflict
- The importance of staying in control

GETTING ANGRY

An important part of being human is showing our feelings. There are many different emotions we can have, depending on our mood or the situation we are in. Here are some examples:

HAPPY
AngRy
SAD
CONFUSED
DISAPPOINTED
excited
FRIGHTENED
EMBARRASSED

It's perfectly OK to show how you are feeling but sometimes you need to be careful not to hurt other people. This is especially true when people get angry. Anger can affect people differently. Some people seem to have a 'short fuse' and get angry very easily. Others only seem to get angry after a long time. People get angry for different reasons. Something that makes your teacher really angry might not bother you at all, such as a forgotten homework or lost book. In your relationships with other people, anger is an emotion that needs to be handled carefully.

> **activity...**
>
> **What makes you really angry?**
> Work in a group of about four or five for this activity. You will need a large piece of paper or card and marker pens.
>
> In your group, 'thought shower' what makes you angry. Write your ideas on a large piece of paper. You might choose to present your ideas as a spider diagram – it's up to you.
>
> Your finished page could be displayed or shown to others in the class.

Coping with anger

It is not wrong to get angry, but it is important how you cope with your feelings. You might find a person has upset you so much that you want to hit them or say something hurtful. These reactions are not a solution and can get you into trouble or make you feel even worse afterwards.

Here are some positive ways to express anger:

1. Talk to someone who will understand how you are feeling.
2. Spend some time on your own until you calm down. Go for a walk or go to your room.
3. Do some physical activity, play your favourite sport, or go for a run.
4. Do an activity you enjoy, listen to some music you really like, watch TV or read a book.
5. Punch your pillow or scream at something that won't get upset.
6. Take action! If you are angry because your friend is being bullied, then do something to help.

RELATIONSHIPS

DEALING WITH ARGUMENTS

Everyone has arguments and they can happen for a number of reasons. Perhaps you disagree with what a parent or teacher thinks you should do. Maybe there has been a misunderstanding or you have been accused of doing something. Whatever the reason for the argument, it is important to sort things out because:

- You will feel happier and more relaxed
- You will develop stronger, healthier relationships
- You will feel more positive and have a sense of achievement

Once you have been in an argument, it can be easy to stay angry or upset with the other person. It is important that you communicate with each other. It really does not matter who makes the 'first move'. It is not a sign of weakness or backing down that you are the one who suggests you talk things over. If the other person is violent, insults you or refuses to listen, then you might need someone else to help you resolve the disagreement. If someone acts as a go-between it can help both of you to understand each other's point of view.

STAYING IN CONTROL

When you get into a difficult situation, it is important to stay in control. Someone may have made you really upset or a difference of opinion might have developed into an unpleasant row. Perhaps you have been wrongfully accused of something and need to put across your side of the story. Whatever the situation it is important to keep your cool and avoid losing your temper.

How to cope with conflicts – some practical advice

- **Never lose your temper.** Stay calm and take a deep breath.
- **Be careful what you say.** Do not use abusive language or say hurtful things.
- **Do not use violence.** It will reflect badly on you and could make the situation worse.
- **Listen to what the other person has to say.** There are at least two sides in any dispute or disagreement.
- **Admit when you are wrong.** Be prepared to say sorry, and mean it.
- **Accept an apology.** Don't huff and say it will be a while before you can forgive.
- **Learn to negotiate.** Be prepared to meet someone half way on an issue.

activity... BC WO TPD MI

Read the situations on the CD. They all involve conflict.

1. How would you handle each one? You want to avoid an angry situation and reach an agreement. Write down what you would do on the worksheet. When you have finished, discuss your answers in small groups.

2. Choose one of these situations to role play. Remember to show how you would **stay calm, negotiate** and **avoid conflict**.

16. BOYFRIENDS AND GIRLFRIENDS

We are learning about:
- What girls and boys think of the opposite sex
- Issues with dating relationships
- Possible problems in dating relationships

THINKING ABOUT THE OPPOSITE SEX

As you grow up, you will start to notice that boys and girls are different. Your body will develop and change during puberty and your feelings will probably start to change as well. You might begin to find the opposite sex quite interesting. Boys stop thinking of girls as being weird and girls stop thinking that boys are horrible. Your feelings towards a particular person might change as well, as someone you thought of as 'just a friend' starts to become a bit more special.

For discussion…
What do girls think about boys? What do boys think about girls?

What do girls and boys of your age think about themselves?

activity…

Work in a single-sex group and 'thought shower' the questions in the discussion box. Choose someone in your group to write down your ideas.

- When you have finished, a boys group should compare their ideas to a girls group. Discuss what boys and girls think of each other. Is this accurate?
- If you go to a single sex school, your teacher might ask you to survey some of your friends and family for homework.

GOING OUT TOGETHER

There are many different kinds of love – love for your family, love for your friends, love for your pets and even love for your favourite places, things and food! There is a type of love that becomes more and more important as you grow and develop. This is the special feeling that makes you find somebody attractive. A young person might begin a dating relationship when they start thinking about another person in this way. These are the feelings that will eventually lead you to 'fall in love' with someone. Dating can be a fun and exciting part of your life, but it can also be very confusing as you get used to handling new feelings. Dating relationships can be very upsetting if things go badly, or if you feel let down by someone.

When is the right age to start dating?

There is no set age at which to start dating. Everyone is different and will be ready for a dating relationship at a different time. A dating relationship should happen when you are ready and when your parents and carers are OK with it too. Different families will have their own rules about dating and your family may think you are too young at the moment. When you start a dating relationship, it should also be because you care about someone, not because all your friends are dating.

RELATIONSHIPS

At first, the best way to get to know someone of the opposite sex is in a mixed group, rather than going out as a couple. This way you can keep things casual and friendly. When you first start going on dates, it is probably best to date someone fairly close to your own age. It is possible that someone older than you, even by just a year or two, might want a more physical relationship than you do.

What is a healthy dating relationship?
A healthy dating relationship will include all the qualities of a healthy friendship.
Here are some things that are especially important:

- Trust
- Honesty
- Respect
- Good communication

Can you think of any others?

PROBLEMS
When you first begin dating, you probably won't want to get too serious straightaway and will have lots of different boyfriends or girlfriends. You may discover that the person you have been getting to know does not really have enough in common with you. If you decide to end a dating relationship, you should not feel guilty about it. Just remember to be sensitive and choose the right moment to break the news – definitely not in front of a group of friends or just before an exam!

activity...

What advice would you give?
Some of the problems that can happen when young people start dating are shown in these 'Problem page' letters. In pairs, discuss what advice you would give to each person. Choose one letter and write your answer.

HE'S GETTING TOO SERIOUS
I have been out with my boyfriend on a few dates now, but always with other people, which suits me fine. The problem is that he's started going on at me to spend time alone with him. He often baby-sits for his older sister and suggested I go with him. I feel uncomfortable about it but I don't want him to finish with me. What do you think I should do?

What's the matter with me?
All my mates have asked girls out, but no-one seems interested in me. I really like one of the girls in my class and I think she likes me, too. There's a school disco coming up at the end of term. I really want to ask her to go with me, but I am too shy to ask. To make matters worse, my two older brothers keep teasing me about when I am going to start dating. Should I get my friend to ask for me or would this look silly? Please help!

My boyfriend has dumped me for my best friend
One minute we seemed to be getting on really well, and then all of a sudden my boyfriend seemed to go off me. He made some excuses about why he couldn't see me at the weekend, and then sent me a text saying he wanted to finish with me. I have heard a rumour that he has asked my best friend out. What should I do? I don't want to lose him. Should I ask my friend not to go out with him?

WO MI BC TPD

CITIZENSHIP

DIVERSITY AND INCLUSION

HUMAN RIGHTS AND SOCIAL RESPONSIBILITY

EQUALITY AND SOCIAL JUSTICE

DEMOCRACY AND ACTIVE PARTICIPATION

CITIZENSHIP

DIVERSITY AND INCLUSION

1. MY IDENTITY

We are learning about:
- What it means to have identity
- Different groups you have an identity with
- Your place in your community

WHAT IS IDENTITY?

Your identity is an important part of who you are. What activities do you enjoy watching or taking part in? Do you belong to any clubs or play for any teams? Do you have any religious beliefs? The things you like, the groups you belong to and your family background all help to shape your identity.

activity... COM

Bring an object to class that is important to you. Be prepared to explain to the rest of the class, or to a smaller group, what this item says about your identity.

think about... TPD MI SM

Your personal identity is all about who you are as a person. Think about how you would complete the following statements. They are some of the things that help to make up your personal identity.

MY IDENTITY

- **I can…** Everyone is good at something. What are your abilities? Sometimes a person's sense of identity can come from a having a talent or skill.

- **I like…** Your identity can be linked to the things you like. What is your favourite food, leisure activity or subject at school?

- **I have…** The things you own can say a lot about a person. What are your most important possessions? Do they show anything about your identity?

- **I believe…** You might have beliefs because you follow a religion. Some people have beliefs because of their own personal opinion. What beliefs are important to you?

- **I take part in…** Your identity can be linked to the activities you do. What things do you take part in that say something about your identity?

- **I remember…** Your memories are also part of your identity. What events stand out in your life as being especially important to you?

DIVERSITY AND INCLUSION

BELONGING TO A GROUP

Having a sense of group identity is important and it can give you a feeling of belonging. It can be reassuring to know that there are people like you who share your beliefs and background, or who enjoy doing the same things. Belonging to a group can help you to make friends, share interests and learn from other people.

alone and refuse to join in. Sometimes being in a group can give you an identity it is not good to have.

For discussion…
Which groups do you belong to?

Is being a member of this group a good experience for you and for others?

ME IN MY COMMUNITY

Your community is the area in which you live out your daily life. As a young person, your community is probably like this:

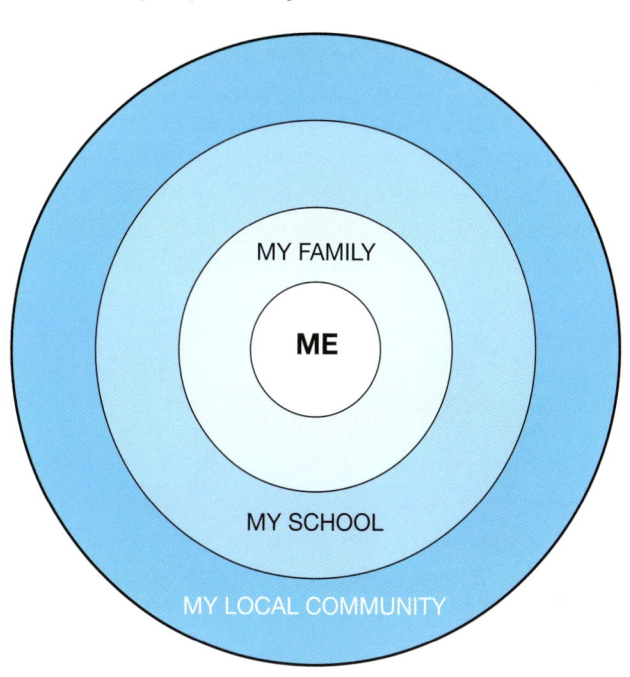

- MY LOCAL COMMUNITY
  - MY SCHOOL
    - MY FAMILY
      - ME

think about…

Why belong to a group?

People are stronger when they are part of a group. A group can offer protection and support for everyone who is a member.

You could easily snap a single stick, but why would a whole bundle be more difficult to break?

You could rip a single sheet of paper in half without any effort, but could you tear a phone directory just as easily?

Are there any other advantages of being part of a group?

Within these main areas, you will probably belong to a number of smaller groups. Your close family will be the people you live with. You may also be part of a larger family group that includes aunts and uncles, cousins and grandparents. In school you will be the member of a class or registration group and probably other groups as well, such as a club or team.

think about…

Within your family, school and local community what groups do you belong to? What does membership of these groups show about your identity?

WHEN BEING IN A GROUP IS A BAD THING…

There are times when being in a group is not a good experience. Groups can sometimes be very threatening to people who do not belong. They can also be exclusive and deliberately make people feel left out. No-one likes to feel that they are not 'good enough' to join a group. Have you ever deliberately left anyone out of a group? It can be very hurtful to feel excluded. If a group of friends have joined together to bully someone, then this is not a good reason to be in a group. In this situation it is better to stand

CITIZENSHIP

2. FAMILY LIFE

We are learning about:
- How families are different to each other
- Family identity
- Growing up in different parts of the world

FAMILIES ARE DIFFERENT

All families have their own way of doing things. You have probably noticed this when you visit a friend's house. The daily routine or meal times might be different and members of the family might have different responsibilities to your family.

The differences can be even greater when a family is from a different background or country. Many families live their lives according to the teachings of a religion. This can affect what foods are eaten and how the meals are prepared, what clothes are worn and what celebrations take place in the family.

FAMILY IDENTITY

Perhaps some of the special practices your family has are because of religion or background. In the same way that you show your identity as an individual, your family also shows identity. Some families may choose to keep themselves separate, but most are part of a larger group or local community. This can have an important influence on family life. It can be good to know that your family identifies with a larger group or community. It can help you to feel safe and confident and give you a feeling of belonging. It can also help you to realise that not every family is the same as yours. This does not make someone else's family strange – just different to yours!

FAMILIES AROUND THE WORLD

Families in different parts of the world will have their own customs and traditions. Children and young people growing up in other countries will probably have a lifestyle that is very different to yours. Every culture in the world has their traditions. These are the ways of doing things that are passed on from parents to children.

Nasreen lives in Pakistan

My name is Nasreen and I am an 11 year old girl. I will tell you about my family. I have three sisters, two brothers, a mother, a father and grandparents. We all live together in the same house. Our home only has one floor and it has a flat roof. We have no running water inside and no electricity. My family are Muslims.

It can get really hot here, especially in the summer when the temperatures can go over 40°C. The men wear baggy pants with a long shirt that hangs down to their knees and the women and girls wear scarves on their heads. Some people in the big cities wear western style clothes.

think about...

What makes your family special?
Think about the way you do things in your family.

Do you have any special family customs or traditions, perhaps at a time of celebration such as someone's birthday? Are there any other times during the year when your family has their own way of doing something?

Talk to the person sitting beside you about what makes your families special.

DIVERSITY AND INCLUSION

I have left school now and stay at home to help my mother and grandmother with the chores. Less than half of the children here get to go to school at all, so I was one of the lucky ones. Boys and girls are always taught separately, as this is one of the rules in the Qu'ran, our holy book. The Qu'ran also tells us what we may or may not eat. Muslims are not allowed anything that comes from a pig and our meat has to come from an animal that has been killed in a special way. At home we often eat vegetables and lamb with a thick, spicy sauce.

Pieter lives in the Netherlands

I live in a small country in Northern Europe called the Netherlands, where we speak Dutch.

My house is near a dyke. This is a wall that stops the sea water from flooding across the land. My country is very flat and we also have nice weather, not too cold in winter and the summers are not too hot, either. We grow lots of flowers here.

I love playing football and it is one of the things I like best at school. I go to school every day during the week. Many children in the Netherlands speak two languages besides Dutch. We learn English in my school and either German or French as well.

I love the holidays and my favourite is Easter. We decorate eggs, then we have a competition where we bump them together to see whose breaks first. Sometimes we also light huge bonfires on a hill or high point. People start to collect wood weeks in advance and each area tries to build the biggest bonfire.

I also enjoy St Nicholas' day on 5 December. We get nice treats to eat, like sweet pastries filled with marzipan and chocolate figures of Sinterklaas (Santa Claus) wrapped in coloured foil.

Shivani lives in Northern Ireland

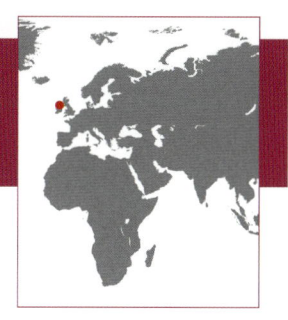

I have lived in Belfast since I was born – that's 12 years, so I think of myself as Northern Irish. My parents came to live here about 20 years ago but I still have grandparents and relatives in India. I am Hindu, like the rest of my family. Sometimes pupils in my school say it must be awful not to have Christmas. Well, Hindus have plenty of celebrations during the year. One of my favourite is Diwali when we decorate our houses with lots of lights, give presents and get treats to eat. I still get Christmas presents for my friends and last Halloween we all went 'trick or treating'. It was great fun!

My family has a really big celebration coming up this year. My sister is getting married and many of my relatives will be visiting from India. The marriage was arranged between my parents and her fiancée's father, and she is very pleased about the arrangement. Some of my friends think this is a strange way of doing things, but it is one of our traditions and it works for us!

activity

Read each of the stories and answer the following questions:

1. How does each of these lives differ to your own?
2. What could be some of the reasons for these differences?
3. Give examples of how each family shows their identity.
4. Is this identity because of where they live, what they believe or something else?

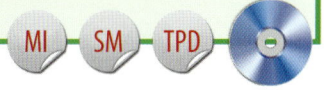

CITIZENSHIP

3. ATTITUDES TO OTHERS

We are learning about:
- What is meant by diversity
- Definitions of key words
- Having a positive attitude to other people

DIFFERENT PEOPLE, DIFFERENT BACKGROUNDS

During your day, you will spend time with people who share your identity. You will also meet people with different identities from different backgrounds. This is known as diversity. What do you think about people who are different to you and how do you treat them? This is an important question. In recent years, many people from other countries and different backgrounds have chosen to make Northern Ireland their home. Everyone needs to be treated fairly and have the same opportunities. Everyone also needs to understand, appreciate and work with people from different backgrounds.

> **activity**
>
> Consider the area in which you live. Do the buildings or businesses nearest to your home suggest that there are people from different backgrounds in the local community? On your way to school make a note of as many examples as you can. Produce a map to show examples of diversity in your local area.

NEGATIVE ATTITUDES

Have you ever thought someone was strange or scary because they looked different or liked to eat food you had never heard of? Remember that they might think the same about you! We should not think badly about people from other backgrounds just because they are different. It is also not fair to judge people from other countries before getting to know them. The following words refer to some of the ways in which people might treat others unfairly:

Prejudice

The word 'prejudice' literally means to 'pre-judge' someone. If a person shows prejudice they have made up their mind about someone or something before they know the facts. Prejudice is therefore a negative idea or attitude that someone has.

Stereotyping

A stereotype is a mental picture that a person might have of someone from a different background. Stereotyping someone means assuming that everyone from a certain group has the same characteristics.

Discrimination

Discrimination occurs when someone is not treated fairly or equally. Sometimes people treat others in this way because they have a prejudiced attitude or have stereotyped someone in a certain way. Discrimination means to put prejudiced ideas into action.

Racism

Racism is the belief that people of a different race are inferior or unequal to others and should not be treated fairly. Racism can involve discrimination because of a person's skin colour, the language they speak or the country where they were born.

Sectarianism

Sectarianism is prejudice or discrimination towards someone who is a member of a smaller group within the same race or nationality. In Northern Ireland, this term is often used to describe prejudice between Protestants and

DIVERSITY AND INCLUSION

Catholics. They are both part of the same religion but have some different beliefs and practices.

UNDERSTANDING
RESPECT
TOLERANCE
FAIRNESS
EQUALITY
ACCEPTANCE
BELONGING
WELCOMING

For discussion…
Work in groups of about four.

What are some of the advantages for everyone when people from different backgrounds live in the same area?

What difficulties could there be?

How could problems be overcome?

For discussion…
What do each of the words in the box above mean?

How can you, your school and your community try to overcome discrimination and help everyone feel valued?

POSITIVE ACTION
It is important that everyone feels welcomed and that their background is valued.
Here are some ways that could help you to understand people from different backgrounds:

DOs
- Find out what you have in common. Someone in your class might follow a different religion to your own, but do they enjoy the same sports or hobbies as you?
- Find out more about the differences. It can be really interesting to find out why people do things differently. What are the reasons for the special diet or different clothes?

DON'Ts
- Don't judge people before you get to know them or blame someone unfairly. Remember how you like to be treated by others!
- Don't be put off making friends with someone because their cultural background is different to yours.

activity…
Carry out a survey in your class or year group of how many different racial or religious groups there are.

Produce a group poster where each group is represented in words or pictures.

activity…
Find out what your school does to make pupils from other cultures and backgrounds feel welcome.

What more could be done?

Share your ideas with others in your class.

CITIZENSHIP

HUMAN RIGHTS AND SOCIAL RESPONSIBILITY

4. WHAT ARE HUMAN RIGHTS?

We are learning about:
- What human rights are
- The difference between needs and wants
- The UN Declaration on Human Rights

RIGHTS FOR EVERYONE

A basic need for humans is called a human right. All people everywhere should have what they need. This means more than just enough air, food and water to survive. Some human rights are concerned with physical needs, such as decent housing and health care. Others refer to the right of each person to have their own opinions or follow a religion if they choose to. A human right is something that all people everywhere deserve just because they are human. You do not have to earn human rights and they are available to everyone, not just the people who can afford to pay for them. Human rights should not be denied to anyone because of factors such as race, religion, colour or nationality. Most countries promise that they will try and make sure that all their citizens have human rights.

think about...

What does it mean to be fully human?

How is this different from just 'surviving' or simply 'being alive'?

What are some of the things humans need in order to live happy and contented lives?

NEEDS AND WANTS

When looking at rights, it is important to think about the difference between **needs** and **wants**. A need is something you must have for survival, such as food, water or shelter. A want is something you would like to have such as an ipad or a better phone. Some items can be both a need and a want. For example, food is needed for survival, but some sweets at lunchtime would be a want rather than a need. Clothes are also essential, but they do not have to be the latest fashion or have a designer label. Sometimes an item could be considered both a need and a want depending on your lifestyle or where you live. For example, many people consider Internet access to be a need, while many other people in the world do not even have electricity in their homes.

For discussion…
Are the following needs or wants?
- clean water
- bread
- designer jeans
- computer
- books
- medical care
- nutritious food
- holiday trips
- following your religion
- giving your opinion
- being listened to
- sweets
- fast food
- X box

For discussion…
Working with a partner, make a list of five needs that everyone should have. Join with another pair and compare your lists. Combine them to make a new list of needs that everyone agrees with.

Discuss the following questions in your group and refer to the list of needs you have agreed on. Your teacher may ask you to report back to the rest of the class.

- Is it easy to decide whether something is a need or a want?
- What can happen to someone if they do not receive their basic needs?

HUMAN RIGHTS AND SOCIAL RESPONSIBILITY

- Is it fair that some people have their wants satisfied while others do not have their basic needs met?
- Are there people who do not have their basic needs met in Northern Ireland, in your local community or in your school? Give examples.
- Should these needs be met? If so, why?
- Whose responsibility is it to make sure people's needs are met?

FOCUS ON THE UDHR

The United Nations is an international group of people with members from most countries. After the suffering of the Second World War, many people realised there was a need to protect human rights. In 1948, the UN produced the Universal Declaration of Human Rights (UDHR). It describes the rights all humans should have, no matter where they live or who they are. The UDHR contains 30 articles or statements describing the rights which every person should receive. All the rights are equal to each other and it is the responsibility of governments to promote them.

activity...

Look at a simplified version of the UDHR on the CD.

Which articles (statements) in the declaration do you think are the most important?

Do any of the five basic needs your group agreed on appear as articles in the declaration?

MAKING PROMISES ... BREAKING PROMISES

What promises did you make last week? Perhaps you told a parent or carer that you would keep your room tidy or that you would not annoy your brother or sister. Maybe you promised a teacher that you would sort out your notes or hand in a late homework.

Did you make any promises to your friends? It is important to try and keep promises, but sometimes it can be difficult.

think about...

What promises do you find hard to keep? Which ones are easy?

Countries sign up to the UDHR to show that they promise to protect people's rights. Sometimes, these promises are broken. A government may do this deliberately and ignore an article in the UDHR. When this happens it is called a violation of human rights. In some countries, the government is not able to provide for all its citizens, perhaps because of poverty, war or a natural disaster.

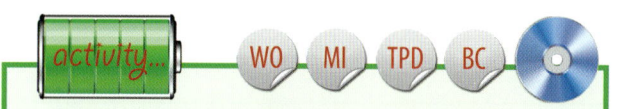

activity...

HUMAN RIGHTS TREE

Work in a group of about four for this activity.

- Draw a tree on a large piece of paper or use the worksheet from the CD.
- Take it in turns to write on the tree (as leaves, fruits or flowers) the human rights that are needed for all people to live happy, safe and fulfilled lives.
- A tree needs roots to grow and flourish. Draw roots on your tree and label them with the things that help human rights to flourish. For example, good education, a respect for law and order or a healthy economy.
- When your drawing is complete, match your leaves, fruits or flowers to an article of the UDHR. Write the number of the article on your drawing.
- You could show your tree to the rest of the class and explain reasons for the items you have included.

CITIZENSHIP

5. CHILDREN'S RIGHTS

We are learning about:
- The need for children's rights
- The UN Convention on the Rights of the Child
- Children and the law

SPECIAL PROMISES FOR CHILDREN

Children are special and extra care needs to be taken with their rights. World leaders decided that children needed rights just for them as they are less physically and mentally mature than adults. Children are usually smaller and more easily threatened than adults because they are younger. The United Nations Convention on the Rights of the Child is a list of rights for children, no matter where they live. Nearly every country in the world has signed the UNCRC to show that it has promised to give young people under the age of 18 years special care and protection.

Every five years, the government of a country has to give a report to a group of experts in the United Nations saying how they have kept these promises.

The UN Convention on the Rights of the Child has 54 articles. Each article is a statement saying what rights children have and how they should be protected. Here are some simplified examples:

Article 4 Governments must do all they can to protect children's rights.
Article 6 Every child has the right to be alive and to be the best person they can be.
Article 8 Governments must protect the child's right to a name, a nationality and a family life.
Article 12 Every child has the right to express his or her views, and those views must be taken seriously.
Article 14 Every child has the right to have his or her own beliefs and religion.
Article 16 The law must protect every child's right to privacy.
Article 17 Governments must make sure children get lots of different information about all sorts of things. They should protect children from harmful information.
Article 18 Governments must support parents. Parents must always try to do what is best for children.
Article 19 Every child must be protected from all forms of violence, abuse, neglect and bad treatment.
Article 23 Disabled children have the right to a full life, and to be part of the community.
Article 24 Every child has the right to the best possible health.
Article 28 Every child has the right to education.
Article 31 Every child has the right to rest, play and to do things they enjoy.
Article 32 Children must be protected from harmful work.
Article 33 Governments must do everything to protect children from illegal drugs.
Article 36 Governments must protect children from all other harm.
Article 37 Every child has the right to protection from torture and very bad treatment.
Article 38 Children must be protected from wars and from joining the armed forces.
Article 42 Governments must tell everyone about all the rights in this Convention.

activity...

Work in groups of about four or five for this activity.

You will be given cards from the CD showing each article in the UNCRC.

Work together to choose the 20 articles you think are the most important.

Next, reduce your group of 20 cards to 10, and then decide on a final 5.

HUMAN RIGHTS AND SOCIAL RESPONSIBILITY

For discussion …
Staying in your groups, discuss the following:

1. Why did you decide on these 5 articles?
2. Which of the following areas have been covered by your final choice?
   - Views and opinions
   - Family life
   - Health and well-being
   - Education and leisure
   - Protection from harm
3. How does your choice compare with other groups in the class?
4. Do you think that the promises in the UNCRC are enough to make sure all the children of the world are properly cared for and protected?
5. What would you do to improve children's rights?

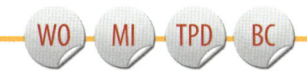

WO MI TPD BC

CHILDREN AND THE LAW

The UN Convention on the Rights of the Child shows that children are entitled to human rights as well as adults. It shows that children need special protection, too. A person does not have full adult rights until they reach 18 years of age. Under the law, a child does not have the same rights to goods and services as an adult, for example, they cannot buy alcohol legally or watch an adult film in the cinema. The law works to protect children and young people, not to deny their rights!

At what age can I…

Here are some examples of the law for children and young people in Northern Ireland:

Get a part time job? At 13 years of age, but there are a number of restrictions. For example, you cannot work more than 2 hours on a school day nor do any paid work when you are supposed to be in school.

Buy a pet? Legally you can buy a pet once you are 12 years old but it is advisable to ask your parents' or carers' permission first!

Get a piercing? There is no legal age, but children need the consent of a parent or carer.

Do you think this little girl is too young to have her ears pierced?

Smoke? You have to be over 18 to buy cigarettes or tobacco. If you smoke in public and look under 18 years of age, a police officer can confiscate your cigarettes.

Buy alcohol? You can buy and drink alcohol when you are 18 years of age.

Get a tattoo? It is illegal for someone under the age of 18 to have a tattoo, even with the consent of their parents.

Buy fireworks? You must be 16 years old to buy fireworks. You must also buy a licence.

Be held responsible for a crime? At age 10 you can be charged with a crime and sent to a young person's detention centre.

Open a bank account? You can open a bank account in your own name from the age of 7.

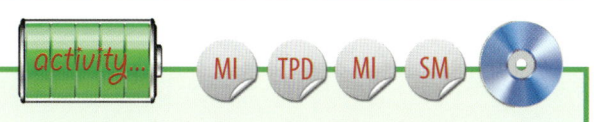

activity… MI TPD MI SM

How much do you know about the law and children's rights? See how you score in the quiz on the CD.

CITIZENSHIP

6. WHERE RIGHTS ARE DENIED

We are learning about:
- Street children
- Child labourers
- What action is being taken

STREET CHILDREN

In many countries, children live on the streets with no home and no one to care for them. They are one of the groups of people most likely to be denied their rights. Children end up on the streets for many different reasons, but the most common one is poverty. Many parents worldwide are too poor to support their family so a child might be turned out of the house. Sometimes children suffer such abuse at home that they have to run away. Other children live on the streets because they are orphans and there is no-one to look after them. Their parents may have been killed by conflict or HIV/AIDS.

Some children live on the streets during the day but return to their families at night. They will spend their day begging or working. They might earn money by shining shoes, cleaning car windscreens or looking through rubbish for items to sell. These children cannot go to school. Their parents have to send them on to the streets each day as they need the money. Some children also have to work in this way to support a parent who is addicted to drugs or alcohol.

Problems faced by street children

Here are some of the many problems faced by children living on the streets:

Poor health – Street children often live and work on rubbish dumps or in sewers. They do not receive their vaccinations and are unlikely to see a doctor when they are ill.

Not enough food – Many street children are very underweight. Their only food is what they can beg, steal or find in other people's rubbish.

Violence – Street children often have no-one to protect them from harm. In some countries they are beaten or even killed by the police as they are seen as a nuisance.

No education – For street children, there is no chance of going to school, but also little opportunity to relax or play.

> **activity** — WO MI TPD
>
> Work with a partner.
> You have been learning about the rights that everyone should have, especially children.
> Make a list of the conditions children may have to face if they live on the streets or are forced into child labour. Try to match each one with a right that all children should have.

CHILD LABOUR

Many children worldwide do some form of paid work. Maybe you help around the house in return for pocket money or look after a younger brother or sister. You will soon be old enough for a part time job, such as a paper round. This sort of work is not child labour. When work is harmful then it is called 'child labour' and is a cause for concern. Children should not have to do work if it prevents them getting an education, puts them in danger or stops them from having a normal family life.

HUMAN RIGHTS AND SOCIAL RESPONSIBILITY

What jobs do children do?
Many children sell things, such as fruit they have picked or items taken from a rubbish tip or bin. Other common jobs for children are collecting firewood, looking after animals or working in someone's house as a domestic servant. Sometimes children have to work in dangerous conditions, lifting heavy loads or using harmful chemicals. Children should be protected from war, but sometimes children as young as seven years old are forced to fight in armed conflicts. Factories in the developing world often use children as their small hands are suited to delicate work. Child labourers are very badly treated, working long hours for very little pay.

Is child labour a serious problem?
Here are some facts and figures:
- One in six children aged 5 to 14 years old (about 16% of all children in this age group) is involved in child labour in developing countries.
- In the least developed countries, 30% of all children are engaged in child labour.
- Worldwide, 126 million children work in hazardous conditions, often enduring beatings and humiliation by their employers.
- An estimated 1.2 million children, both boys and girls, are sold as slaves each year into work in agriculture, mining, factories, armed conflict or prostitution.

Figures from: www.unicef.org, www.ilo.org, www.crin.org

RAJESH'S STORY
Rajesh lives in India.
This is his story.

My mother had taken us to live with my grandmother to escape my father. One day my mother left my grandmother's house without me and never came back. My grandmother would go to work every day in Kolkata as a domestic help and I was left alone. I would go from place to place to try and get food. I would cry a lot. I never went to school.
I was eight years old when I ran away.

I ended up at Sealdah train station in Kolkata. I went to work with a lime juice vendor in the station. A gang of boys who were drug abusers would take all the money I earned from the juice vendor. So I found my own group who did not take drugs – we ate together and slept together to stay safe.

When I was in Sealdah, I saw many children who had no parents, no food, who were forced to work at different jobs. I felt very sad looking at all these things. I would see children beaten because they broke a cup or didn't wash a utensil properly. Then another boy took me to a drop-in centre run by CINI Urban Unit (ChildHope's local partner organisation). I started staying in the centre, day and night. I stopped my job. I was still not ten years old.

I study every day here and have time to play. My favourite sports are football and cricket. If I get a good result in my tests, CINI Urban Unit will help me to go to boarding school. I would like to work as a car mechanic. Maybe I can help children living on the street or on the platforms. Now I am getting good meals every day and I am in a secure environment. If it wasn't for CINI Urban Unit, I would have done nothing. Now I want to do something for myself.

Rajesh's story is from ChildHope, www.childhope.org.uk, a charity dedicated to supporting street and working children to transform their futures.

activity... SM MI TPD

Use the Internet to research an organisation that is taking action to stand up for street children or child labourers.

You could present your findings in the form of an illustrated report or PowerPoint.

BC ICT

CITIZENSHIP

EQUALITY AND SOCIAL JUSTICE
7. IT'S NOT FAIR!

We are learning about:
- The importance of fair treatment
- How some groups of people face discrimination
- The laws which protect people

PROTECTING PEOPLE'S RIGHTS

You have probably grumbled from time to time about something not being fair. Perhaps a teacher has set too much homework or maybe it seems as if a brother or sister gets a better deal than you. Complaints like these usually get ignored! However, in our society nowadays, people are very concerned about what is right and fair. No-one should experience discrimination or unjust treatment. However, many people still feel that they are not treated fairly. The problem can be that other people's attitudes still need to change.

The Law in Northern Ireland

The Good Friday Agreement was signed in April 1998. It was part of the peace process that brought an end to 'the troubles' at the end of the last century. As part of this agreement, new laws were put in place with the Northern Ireland Act. Section 75 of this act is all about equality. There are nine different groups of people covered by these laws. We shall look at how three of these groups might be excluded in society and how the law can protect them.

DISABILITY

A person who is disabled might be someone with reduced sight, hearing, speech or mobility. Disability can also include a mental health or a learning difficulty. Many disabled people face discrimination. They may struggle to get onto public transport, get into buildings, go to school with their friends or find work. Many people with a learning disability are treated as 'different' and they face challenges and prejudice everyday. Disabled people want to be accepted for who they are and do not want to feel excluded from society.

People with disabilities have their rights protected by law in the **Disability Discrimination Act of 1995,** the **Human Rights Act 1998** and **Section 75 of the Northern Ireland Act 1998.** These laws give people protection from unfair treatment at school or work, on public transport and in places like shops and cinemas. For example, a taxi driver could not charge extra money for taking a guide dog.

> **think about...** SM | MI | TPD | WO
>
> Why do some disabled people face prejudice and discrimination, even though there are laws in place to protect their rights?
>
> Read the situations on the CD. Do they show fair or unfair treatment of a disabled person?

RACIAL GROUP

People from many different backgrounds live in Northern Ireland. Many members of the Chinese and Indian communities have been here for generations now and more recently, people from Eastern European countries have chosen to make Northern Ireland their home. It is important that no one feels excluded because of his or her race.

Most people find Northern Ireland a friendly and welcoming place in which to live. However, there is a minority who make life unpleasant for people from a different racial background. Racist

EQUALITY AND SOCIAL JUSTICE

attacks on people's homes and businesses include damage to property and threatening graffiti. A recent report has found that racial bullying is a serious problem in some schools in Northern Ireland.

The Race Relations Order 1997 has made it illegal to treat someone unfairly because of colour, race, nationality or ethnic origin. The law covers school, the workplace and the community. For example, you cannot be refused a hotel room or a table in a restaurant because of your race. The Irish Traveller community is protected from discrimination. The law recognises that they are a racial group.

> **activity...** MI TPD WO
>
> Read the news item on the CD and discuss the questions with a partner.

> **activity...** BC MI SM ICT COM
>
> Design a poster or leaflet. Imagine it is to be used or displayed in your school (perhaps at an open evening). Your aim is to show new pupils that everyone is welcomed and valued. You could use a computer for this activity.

AGE

Age discrimination is when you are treated unfairly because of your age. Some people think this is more of a problem for older people. However, many children and young people also face age discrimination. **Section 75 of the Northern Ireland Act** says people should be given equality regardless of their age.

> A survey carried out in 2010 showed that:
> - Around half of children and young people experienced age discrimination.
> - 49% of 7–17 year olds said they have been treated unfairly because of their age.

> - A quarter of 7–17 years olds said they are treated unfairly during everyday activities such as shopping or using public transport.
> - Around one in five experienced discrimination while visiting a café or using local sports facilities.
>
> Figures from: www.headsup.org.uk

> **For discussion...** TPD WO
>
> Have you ever experienced discrimination because of your age?
> How did it make you feel?
> What action (if any) did you take?

Jessica Robinson, a teenager, explains the reasons why she set up an anti-discrimination Facebook group:

"I set up my Against The Discrimination and Mistreatment of Teenagers Facebook group out of frustration of not being allowed into shops in my school uniform, security guards constantly following me around and the Mosquito* in my local area, which was forever bugging me!"

* Note: The mosquito is an electronic noise, used to prevent young people from hanging around outside.

Find out more about Jessica's campaign against age discrimination and other similar cases at http://www.crae.org.uk/protecting/age-discrimination.html

> **activity...** MI SM ICT
>
> Use the Internet to find examples of people feeling excluded because of disability, race or age. What action could be taken? Share your examples with the rest of the class.

CITIZENSHIP

8. NOWHERE TO CALL HOME

We are learning about:
- What it means to be homeless
- Why people become homeless
- The work of organisations tackling homelessness

HOMELESSNESS

"What is homelessness?"
Quite simply, being homeless means that you do not have a home. It doesn't just mean sleeping rough or living on the streets. Even if you have a roof over your head, you can still be homeless. If you are living in temporary accommodation or staying with friends or relatives in an emergency, you are still homeless.

My Experience of Homelessness
John's Story
"After months of family conflict I finally left home and went to stay with some friends. After a while I felt that I was imposing because I thought that I was constantly in the way, so I left. I phoned my brother for advice and he told me to go to a hostel. The first hostel I went to had no beds, so I got a list of other places and went from there."

Back to Independence
Stephen's Story
"I am 22 years old and have been living with the Simon Community for almost 2 years now. Becoming homeless was something that I never really thought about until it happened to me. Up until then I had quite a good life. I was brought up by my grandparents who were really good to me. When I was 17 they both became quite ill and I spent most of my time nursing them. By the time I was 19 they had both, sadly, passed away."

Source: www.simoncommunity.org

activity...
Why did John and Stephen become homeless? The CD contains their full stories with a worksheet.

WO MI TPD

"Why do people become homeless?"
There are many reasons why someone can become homeless. A breakdown in relationships is often one of the main causes. Difficult relationships at home can lead to a young person running away or leaving. With no family support, they may become homeless. Sometimes a divorce or separation could lead to homelessness. A person could lose their home because of money problems, perhaps caused by unemployment. Having an addiction problem can also lead to homelessness.

"What problems do homeless people face?"
Without somewhere safe and comfortable to live, it can be very difficult to keep a job or have healthy relationships with others. People are more likely to have poor health or develop an addiction problem. Homeless families living in temporary accommodation have difficult and uncertain lives. Children may find it hard to keep up with their schoolwork, they are unlikely to have a proper place to play and may not be able to see their friends.

EQUALITY AND SOCIAL JUSTICE

Shelter case study 2012

"I feel very sad that me and my brother will have to spend another Christmas in the hostel. I don't know how much I can take. Is it too much to ask for a house?"

13 year old Ashley

"We were suddenly told to leave and had to get our stuff out of the house in one day. It was a Sunday and there were no vans available to hire so we had to call my mum's friend who had a van for catering and we used that.

The whole family had to come down with their cars so we could get our stuff out in time. Even then we had to leave loads of our toys and games. It was horrible grabbing what we could and leaving behind all this stuff."

12 year old Rory

Shelter helps over a million people a year struggling with bad housing or homelessness – and they campaign to prevent it in the first place. They're here so no-one has to fight bad housing or homelessness on their own.

homeless households with 6,000 of these being families with children. Statistics also show that homeless has been increasing in Northern Ireland over the last 10 years.

Statistics from:
http://www.poverty.org.uk/i81/index.shtml

TAKING ACTION ON HOMELESSNESS

One of the most basic human rights is having somewhere safe and comfortable to live. There is concern that in the UK and Ireland today, some people do not have this right. There are a number of organisations helping homeless people. They provide emergency accommodation, offer advice about benefits and work, and give support when someone is able to find a home of their own.

think about... [TPD]

Homelessness can happen to anyone. If your family suddenly became homeless and you had to pack away all your things, what would you miss most? What would be some of the problems of living in temporary accommodation?

"Is homelessness a problem in Northern Ireland?"

Although you may not see people sleeping rough in your local area, homelessness is still a serious problem. Many people do not have a permanent home of their own. They may be in temporary accommodation, living in a hostel or sleeping on a friend's settee. In 2009/10, there were 19,000

activity... [TPD] [ICT] [COM]

Choose one of the following organisations.
- Simon Community NI
  www.simoncommunity.org
- Shelter
  www.shelter.org.uk
- Salvation Army
  www.salvationarmy.org.uk
- Depaul Ireland
  www.depaulireland.org

Visit their website to find out more about what they do. Write a report about how this organisation is tackling the problem of homelessness or poor housing. Your teacher may ask you to share your information with the rest of the class.

[SM] [MI]

CITIZENSHIP

9. FOCUS ON THE BRITISH RED CROSS

British Red Cross

We are learning about:
- The aims of the British Red Cross
- How the organisation started
- Humanitarian work at home and overseas

The British Red Cross is an organisation that helps people in crisis, whoever and wherever they are. They help vulnerable people at home and overseas prepare for and respond to emergencies. When the crisis is over, they help people to recover and move on with their lives. The Red Cross is a humanitarian organisation. This means it is concerned with people's safety and well-being. It takes action to save lives and to stop suffering. It acts impartially, treating people only on the basis of need. Volunteers play an important part in its work.

RED CROSS: THE FACTS
In 2011 the British Red Cross:

- Launched seven emergency appeals, raising £21.6m to help people around the world recover from famine, flooding, conflict and earthquakes.
- Helped 75,000 people in earthquake-hit Haiti recover their livelihoods through cash distribution, and gave 22,000 families in the country safe and improved shelter.
- Responded to 4,200 emergency call outs in the UK, ranging from fires and power cuts to bomb alerts.
- Loaned out 75,000 wheelchairs to help people stay independent.
- Supported 397,000 people in the UK with health and social care services.
- Helped 35,000 refugees and asylum seekers adapt to life in the UK.
- Provided 30,000 people with first aid at 9,000 public events across the UK.
- Gave 6.4m people information about first aid through their campaigns.
- Taught 183,300 people about humanitarian issues through their education programmes.

All figures are taken from the British Red Cross 2011 trustees' report and accounts: www.redcross.org.uk/annualreport

HOW THE RED CROSS BEGAN
The International Red Cross and Red Crescent Movement started in 1863, by a Swiss businessman called Henry Dunant. He was shocked by the suffering of men left to die on the battlefield. He recommended that groups of volunteers could be trained to help those suffering in times of war. This help would be given to everyone in need. Henry Dunant also suggested that countries should have an international agreement to help anyone wounded in battle. This agreement was the original Geneva Convention, adopted in 1864.

In 1870, a society with similar aims was formed in Britain and in 1905 it became known as the British Red Cross. Today, the British Red Cross works at home and overseas as part of the International Red Cross and Red Crescent Movement.

THE EMBLEM OF THE RED CROSS
The red cross has arms of equal length and it is on a white background. It is a symbol of neutral protection in wartime. In many countries where most of the population is Muslim, a red crescent is used instead. However, neither emblem has any religious or political significance.

The neutral protective emblems of the red cross and the red crescent

THE RED CROSS WORKING OVERSEAS
The British Red Cross helps victims of conflicts and disasters. Recent examples include the Haiti earthquake and Pakistan floods of 2010,

EQUALITY AND SOCIAL JUSTICE

the drought in Somalia in 2011 and the West African food crisis of 2012. Here are some of the ways in which the Red Cross provides help:

- **Preparing for disasters** – The Red Cross does not wait for a disaster to happen, they help people to be prepared. It may not be possible to stop a disaster, but being prepared makes a huge difference in saving lives and protecting people's livelihoods.

- **Responding to disasters** – There are few organisations that can respond as quickly as the Red Cross. Their emergency response units are on call 24/7, ready to go anywhere in the world with relief items.

- **Recovering from disasters** – The Red Cross doesn't just provide emergency relief. They stay long after a disaster to help people rebuild their lives.

- **Finding missing family members** – Imagine what it would be like to survive a disaster only to discover that members of your family were missing. When families are separated through a conflict or disaster, the Red Cross works through a global network to put them back in touch – wherever they are.

- **Helping refugees** – Being forced to leave your home and arriving in a new country can be a very difficult experience. The Red Cross helps in a wide number of ways. Some refugees need emergency supplies, others need help to settle in and some friendly advice.

Red Cross and Red Crescent working overseas
Source: the International Federation of Red Cross and Red Crescent Societies (IFRC)

THE RED CROSS WORKING IN THE UK
Health and social care

The British Red Cross gives short term support to people who need help. Someone might be recovering from an operation, or need support in coping at home. Volunteers can help by collecting prescriptions or doing some shopping. This support service helps people to settle into a routine and regain their confidence. The Red Cross also run a medical equipment service. People can borrow a wheelchair, walking frame or other equipment. This helps them return to their own home after a stay in hospital or surgery.

British Red Cross health and social care
Source: Antony Upton/British Red Cross

First Aid

The British Red Cross wants people to feel confident and willing to give people first aid. They run a range of courses for members of the public. The Red Cross promote first aid and road safety to young people. They believe every child should know how to cope in an emergency, and be able to keep themselves safe.

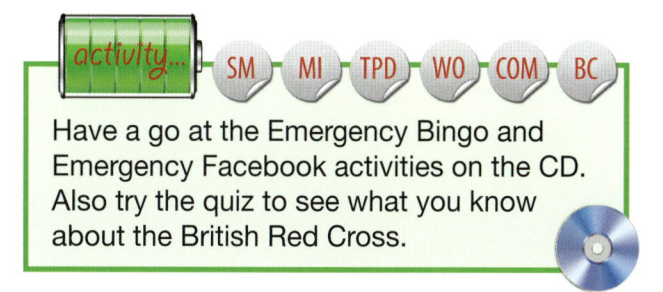

activity... SM MI TPD WO COM BC

Have a go at the Emergency Bingo and Emergency Facebook activities on the CD. Also try the quiz to see what you know about the British Red Cross.

Colourpoint Educational wishes to thank the British Red Cross Society for authorisation to use the Red Cross and Red Crescent emblems and names in this publication.

The British Red Cross, as a member of the International Red Cross and Red Crescent Movement, is a strictly neutral humanitarian organisation. In order to enjoy the confidence of all, Red Cross and Red Crescent organisations do not engage at any time in controversies of a political or ideological nature. The red cross and red crescent emblems are themselves signs of neutrality and protection.

CITIZENSHIP

10. FOCUS ON UNICEF

We are learning about:
- The aims of UNICEF
- UNICEF's role in protecting children's rights
- UNICEF's work in the UK and overseas

WHAT IS UNICEF?
UNICEF is the world's leading organisation focusing on children. For over 60 years, UNICEF has been helping children to survive and thrive from childhood to adolescence. UNICEF works with families, communities and governments in more than 190 countries worldwide to protect and promote the rights of all children. UNICEF is the only organisation mentioned in the **UN Convention on the Rights of the Child** as a source of expert help who can give advice to governments about children's rights.

UK work
UNICEF UK is a registered charity raising funds and awareness to support UNICEF's work worldwide. UNICEF UK campaign to make sure that children everywhere receive their rights. They run programmes in hospitals, schools and local communities in the UK. UNICEF UK works in parliament to protect child rights. Their public affairs team is active in trying to change government policies that do not support children's rights. They make sure that child rights issues are frequently raised in parliament, so MPs can put things right for children in the UK and internationally.

> UNICEF UK's Young Supporters website helps young people get involved with children's rights.
> Visit http://www.unicef.org.uk/youth to find out how you can take action.

WHAT DOES UNICEF BELIEVE?
- Every child has the right to the best possible start in life.
- All children have the same rights.
- It is possible to give every child a good start in life.
- Children's opinions should be listened to.

UNICEF believes that every child has the right to clean water, health care, nutritious food and a safe environment. It is wrong for children to die needlessly because they do not have these things. Children must also be protected from violence and discrimination. All children have the same rights, regardless of their ethnic background, gender, beliefs or background. UNICEF believes that protecting the rights of every child is the surest way to end poverty and bring peace. The world can, if it chooses, make sure that every child grows and develops to their full potential. Children are citizens of their communities and their voices should be heard.

Source: UNICEF

The UN Convention on the Rights of the Child

In 1989, governments worldwide promised all children the same rights by agreeing to the UNCRC. These rights are based on what a child needs to survive, grow, participate and achieve their potential. They apply equally to every child, regardless of who they are, or where they are from.

The convention gives a specific role to UNICEF, as the UN organisation responsible for the rights of children. UNICEF has to promote the convention and encourage governments to keep to it.

EQUALITY AND SOCIAL JUSTICE

The UNCRC guarantees every child the same rights: to an education, to a childhood, to be healthy, to be treated fairly and to be heard. UNICEF works in all these areas to give the best possible outcomes for children.

WHAT DOES UNICEF DO?
Here are some examples of UNICEF's work:

Health care
UNICEF workers distribute life-saving equipment, such as water kits and mosquito nets. They provide support and training for parents and health workers. Today, more children than ever are being immunised against killer diseases.

Education
Every child has the right to an education which develops their personality, talents and abilities to the full. However, more than 100 million children, the majority of them girls, are still denied the right to go to school. UNICEF is working to make sure each primary school child receives an education.

Protecting children
Many children are neglected or hurt, forced to do dangerous work or have to live on the streets. UNICEF works to protect children who are being denied their rights.

Working in emergencies
When an emergency strikes, UNICEF staff in the area act quickly. Emergency specialists assess people's immediate needs, focusing on women and children. UNICEF works long term helping people to rebuild their lives and to improve conditions for children.

WHO DOES UNICEF WORK WITH?
UNICEF helps **governments** to build schools, train teachers and provide textbooks so every child can receive an education. UNICEF also supports governments with health schemes, so every child can be a healthy as possible. They help to train health workers and provide food and clean water.

UNICEF supports **families and communities** to care for children. All children have the right to a childhood, which includes the opportunity to sport and play. No one should abuse children or take advantage of them.

UNICEF aims to involve **children** at every level of decision-making, from school councils to international summits. Children have the right to have their opinions heard.

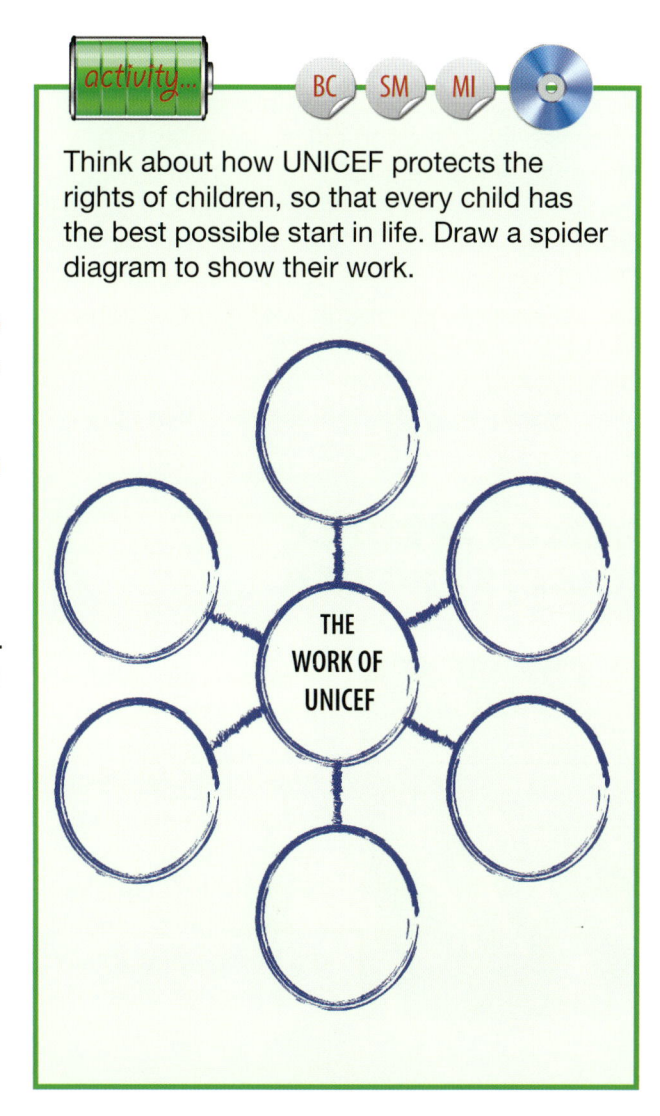

activity... BC SM MI

Think about how UNICEF protects the rights of children, so that every child has the best possible start in life. Draw a spider diagram to show their work.

THE WORK OF UNICEF

DEMOCRACY AND ACTIVE PARTICIPATION

11. WHAT IS A DEMOCRACY?

We are learning about:
- What is meant by democracy
- How Northern Ireland is governed
- People who have responsibility for decision-making

Citizenship is all about the relationship between an individual and the community in which he or she lives. A good citizen behaves in a responsible way in their community, following the law and being considerate to others. A good citizen also takes an active role in their society. One of the ways people can do this, when they are old enough, is through voting in elections.

DEMOCRACY

Our word 'democracy' comes from two Greek words:

DEMOS – PEOPLE
KRATOS – POWER

So democracy means 'power to the people'. This might sound like potential chaos. After all, how can everyone have power and rule their country? Careful organisation is needed. In a democracy, this is done through elections.

Democracy in action

Most schools have a school council or forum, to let teachers and the principal know pupils' opinions on a range of issues. At a council meeting there might be discussion on what could be done to improve the school, especially the facilities for pupils. It would not be practical for everyone in the school to attend a meeting. A class will have an election and vote for a representative. Everyone in the class has the right to vote. They choose the person they think will be the best at representing them. The person who receives the most votes is chosen. This is how a democracy works. Does your school have a council? Perhaps you have already voted for your class representative.

HOW ARE WE GOVERNED?

The decision-making in Northern Ireland is organised on different levels. You would expect the national government to be responsible for the nation's security or how much money people have to pay in taxes. Decisions such as opening hours for the recycling centre or public library are made locally. This way the government can operate more efficiently.

> *Who are these people?*
>
> **MPs** – Members of Parliament are part of the national government and represent us at Westminster.
>
> **MLAs** – These people are members of the Northern Ireland Assembly, our regional government. The letters stand for 'Member of the Legislative Assembly'. The word legislative means the Assembly is able to make laws.
>
> **COUNCILLORS** – These are our local representatives. They meet in the City Hall in Belfast and serve on their local council. Councillors do not work full time and are not paid a wage.

National Government

Northern Ireland is part of the United Kingdom (UK) so decisions made by Parliament in Westminster affect us here. If there is an increase in taxes in the annual budget this will also apply to Northern Ireland. Issues involving other countries are the responsibility of national

DEMOCRACY AND ACTIVE PARTICIPATION

government. Any laws that are passed by the government at Westminster also have to be followed here.

Regional Government

The Northern Ireland Assembly is our Regional Government. It has responsibility for matters that apply to the whole of Northern Ireland. The Assembly can pass laws for the people of Northern Ireland. Its responsibilities include tourism, farming, local industry and policing.

Local Government

Local councils are responsible for issues that concern a smaller area, such as a town or a district. These include rubbish collection and recycling. In Northern Ireland, local government also includes the Education and Library Boards who are responsible for the schools and education in a particular area.

THE NORTHERN IRELAND ASSEMBLY
This is the group of 108 MLAs who are responsible for the day to day running of Northern Ireland. The Assembly has full authority to pass laws. It meets twice a week in the Parliament buildings at Stormont.

THE NORTHERN IRELAND ACT 1998
When the Good Friday Agreement was signed, important new laws were put in place for Northern Ireland. These laws aim to give equality for all people and bring about a more tolerant society.

A CLASS ELECTION

Work in a group of four or five for this activity.

- Your group is a political party. You will need to decide on a name for yourselves.
- There is an election coming up. How are you going to make sure you win?
- Firstly, you will need to decide what issues you think are important. This is called a manifesto. Try to think of things that will appeal to young people, but remember you also need to be realistic.
- You could produce posters or leaflets to help with your campaign.
- Each group then has an election and votes for a party leader. It will be the leader's responsibility to make a speech to the rest of the class about why everyone should vote for your party.
- Finally, there is an election where the class vote for the best party.

Work in groups or four or five for this activity.

Imagine your class are local councillors. Your budget is over-stretched for this year and you must save money by choosing from a range of options.

65

CITIZENSHIP

12. GETTING INVOLVED IN SCHOOL

We are learning about:
- Your school as a community
- How to be more involved in school life
- Ways to be active, help others and have fun

YOUR SCHOOL ENVIRONMENT

Does the school environment matter? Is it acceptable if there is litter everywhere, graffiti in the corridors and broken furniture? If people would not like this at home, then why put up with it in school? You might think the conditions in your school are not your responsibility. However, some pupils deliberately vandalise and graffiti school property making the school environment unpleasant for everyone. This is even worse than not bothering to take responsibility!

activity... COM WO TPD MI BC

SCHOOL SURVEY

Work in groups of four for this activity.

- Your group will be allocated some areas in school. You might need to have a class discussion about which areas should be included in the survey. You have to assess the condition: good, average or poor.
- Each group carries out their survey.
- A spokesperson for your group will share the results of your survey. The whole class then decide on the three areas of the school most in need of improvement.
- Imagine that lottery money is available for school improvement projects. How would you spend the money to improve these areas in your school? Suggest ideas in your group and present them to the rest of the class.

TAKING PART IN SCHOOL LIFE

You are probably still in your first year at your school. Do you take part in any lunchtime or after school clubs, or play for any sports teams? If you have not become involved in activities outside the classroom, why not give something a go? It's a great way to settle in and make friends. Perhaps some of the things other people in your class are doing will give you some ideas. Try something new this week!

activity... WO MI TPD

Write down the ways in which you participate in school. Aim for about five examples. You might like to write your answers on post-it notes.

Here are some suggestions. Perhaps you:

- Play sport, maybe for a team
- Play a musical instrument or sing in the choir
- Take part in class discussions
- Read in assembly
- Are a member of a school club

Share your examples with the rest of the class. If you are using post-it notes, your teacher might display them on the board.

DEMOCRACY AND ACTIVE PARTICIPATION

For discussion...
Discuss the examples given by the class.
- Which is the most popular way of getting involved in school?
- Which is the most original/unusual way?
- Could you participate in more activities? If so, which ones would interest you?
- Is it OK not to be too involved in school life?

COM · MI · TPD · WO

RAISE MONEY FOR CHARITY

Many schools raise money for charity. A whole year group might support a good cause, perhaps by having a non-uniform day. Sometimes a class decides to help a charity or organisation they have been learning about in their lessons. Fundraising can be an excellent way to get involved with school life and with your local community. You could raise money for a charity that is active in your area, or you could support the local branch of a national charity. You could take part in a fundraising event that is already organised, such as a sponsored walk, charity football match or maybe even an abseil or bungee jump! You and some friends could have fun and support a charity at the same time.

Another way that you and your classmates could get involved is to organise your own fundraising event for a good cause. Here are some suggestions:

- Make something that could be sold in school at break time.
- Hold an event that the whole class can take part in, such as a sponsored silence.
- Put on a talent show.
- Organise a disco.
- Have a 'copper collection' where everyone brings in as much small change as they can. It soon mounts up!

activity...
WO · TPD · MI · SM

ORGANISING YOUR EVENT
- Everyone in your class will need to share ideas and discuss:
  1. What charity or organisation are you going to support?
  2. How are you going to raise money?
- You will then need to have a vote to make your final decision.
- Your teacher will need to help with some of the organisation, such as sending home permission slips or dealing with health and safety issues.
- The class might decide to have a committee to take responsibility for some of the planning.
- Finally, after your successful event, you will need to decide how the money will be presented. It might be possible to have a special assembly. You could invite someone from the organisation to come along and give a short talk about how the money will be used.

BC · COM

CITIZENSHIP

13. WHY DO WE NEED RULES?

We are learning about:
- How rules keep people safe
- How rules keep society in good order
- How rules protect human rights

RULES RULE, OK!

Rules are not there to spoil your fun! We need to have rules to follow so everyone can feel safe. Without rules in society, people could take your things, harm you and threaten you, without fear of being punished. Rules are also important at home and in school. You might not agree with every rule your parents, carers or teachers expect you to keep but on the whole, you can probably see that rules are needed to keep people safe and make sure everyone is treated fairly.

activity...

- Write down 10 rules that you have in your school. Here are some examples: no running in the corridor; chewing gum is not allowed; pupils must be in school by 8.45 am.
- Decide on the reason for each rule. Is it there to keep you safe, make sure school runs smoothly or for some other reason?
- Are there any rules in your school that you don't agree with? What are your reasons?
- When you have finished the task, share your ideas with a partner.

For discussion…

Work in a group of two or three.
- What rules do you have at home?
- Why do you have these rules?
- Are there any rules at home that you do not agree with? Why?

THE LAW OF THE LAND

Each country has its own rules that everyone must follow. These are known as 'the law of the land'. These laws are there to protect you and your rights. The law says what your rights are and what duties you have towards other people. The law also states what penalties there are for anyone who breaks the rules.

THE PSNI (The Police Service of Northern Ireland)

The PSNI has an important part to play in making Northern Ireland safer for everyone. They aim to do this by treating everyone fairly and responding quickly if a person has been the victim of a crime. The police have a key role to play in making sure the law is kept by everyone.

Protecting human rights is also an important part of the police's work. The Northern Ireland Policing Board monitors the PSNI to make sure human rights laws are followed. The PSNI also get involved in education. Specially trained police officers go into schools to talk to pupils about many different issues. These include fireworks, alcohol and drugs. The aim of these talks is to promote safety and build links between the police and young people.

DEMOCRACY AND ACTIVE PARTICIPATION

As part of their role in keeping people safe and making sure the law is kept, the police can confiscate anything you are not allowed to have. For example, if you are under 18 years of age and have alcoholic drink or cigarettes in a public place, they can be taken from you.

activity... COM WO BC TPD MI

STRANDED!

Work in a group of about five or six for this activity.

Imagine that your group has survived a plane crash and is stranded in a remote area. There is a small amount of food and bottled water in the plane wreckage, which is nearby. No adults are with you. Discuss what rules you would need to follow until you are rescued.

- Who will decide on the rules?
- Who will make sure everyone keeps the rules?
- What rules will you need to keep everyone safe?
- What rules will you need to make sure everyone is treated fairly?
- How will you deal with anyone who breaks the rules?
- How will you sort out arguments?
- Make a list of your rules and report back to the rest of the class.

PROTECTING HUMAN RIGHTS

You have been looking at how important it is for people of all ages, but especially children, to have their human rights protected. When a country makes promises and signs up to the UN Declaration of Human Rights or Convention on the Rights of the Child, this is a step in the right direction. However, signing something and actually doing something are two different matters. Countries have to show they intend to keep the promises they have made. One way of doing this is for governments to pass laws protecting people's rights.

NICCY

The Northern Ireland Commissioner for Children and Young People works to make sure that the promises in the UNCRC are kept. This involves reminding the government what these promises are. Laws can then be made so children can have their rights protected. NICCY believes it is also important for young people to know what their rights are. They help children and young people do this through new and fun ways to learn about their rights. NICCY also encourages young people to talk to them if they think their rights are being broken.

In 2010, NICCY launched a campaign called **'Make it Right'**. The campaign encourages children and young people to develop their own campaigns on the issues they think are important. NICCY wants the government to listen to young people and value their views.

You can find out more about NICCY from their website:
http://www.niccy.org/Makeitright

CITIZENSHIP

14. TAKING ACTION IN YOUR LOCAL AREA

We are learning about:
- How taking action is everyone's responsibility
- What makes a good neighbour
- Some of the ways to take action in society

Many people are not happy with their neighbourhood. They may feel unsafe due to rising crime or concerned about vandalism or rubbish being dumped. Taking action to improve your local area is something everyone can take responsibility for. Even something simple like not dropping litter or being a good neighbour can make a difference.

> **What makes a good neighbour?**
>
> "I think a good neighbour notices if something is wrong and takes action."
>
> "Good neighbours mind their own business and don't come round complaining if you have your music too loud or play your drum kit in the garage."
>
> "A good neighbour gets involved in the local community and does things to improve the area."
>
> "Good neighbours lend you things when you run out."

How YOU can be a good neighbour…

DOs:
- Keep your pets under control and if your dog leaves a mess, always clean it up.
- Offer to help people who find it hard to do things for themselves, such as elderly neighbours.
- Get involved in community action, such as schemes to tidy up your local area.
- Show respect for other people's property.

DON'Ts:
- Never drop litter or spit your chewing gum onto the pavement.
- Don't play your music so loudly that it annoys the neighbours.
- You should not go onto other people's property without permission.
- Never spray graffiti or vandalise anything – even if it looks derelict and about to be demolished.

Remember, a good neighbour is not just considerate to the people next door, but acts responsibly in the whole neighbourhood!

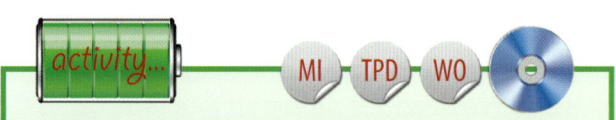

> activity… MI TPD WO
>
> Write down what you think makes someone a good neighbour.

NEWS ITEM

BELFAST TELEGRAPH MAKING THE DIFFERENCE AWARDS

William Dickson was awarded Best Neighbour 2012

He is a "gentleman with a heart of gold" who has worked tirelessly to keep the community spirit alive in south Belfast. Fiercely proud of his roots William Dickson — known as Billy to his neighbours — is a life-long community activist that champions the streets and people he lives around. Billy, a keen historian and tour guide, has worked with young people in the Village area for over 40 years. Speaking up for his neighbours through his role as chairman of the Blackstaff Residents' Association, Billy has the "community's best interests at heart every step of the way" — according to his nomination. Ruth Patterson, who nominated Billy, said: "The Village area in south Belfast is undergoing vast regeneration at this time and Billy is as always ensuring the people of the area are represented and their needs are met for the new housing build.

DEMOCRACY AND ACTIVE PARTICIPATION

"Billy has a heart of gold and is always ready to lend a helping hand no matter how difficult the situation and is a truly deserving recipient to receive a Making the Difference Award."

Source: 'Making the difference 2012: Best Neighbour', *Belfast Telegraph*, 13 December 2011

For discussion…
Why do you think Billy deserved this award?

IMPROVING YOUR LOCAL AREA
Think about the area where you live. Discuss what facilities there are nearby, how safe your neighbourhood is and whether it looks like a nice place to live.

For discussion…
What needs to be done to improve your neighbourhood?

Are there any areas where you can take responsibility?

Facilities
Does your neighbourhood have the services that people need, such as shops and a health centre? Is there anything for young people your age?

Safety
How safe is your local area? Are there a lot of busy main roads or areas where you are not allowed to go?

Appearance
How attractive is the area where you live? Does it look clean and well-cared for or is there a problem with litter or vandalism?

Vandalism
In many areas, vandalism is a serious problem. Sometimes it is public property that gets damaged, such as a bus shelter. Vandals also damage people's homes and cars. Everyone suffers as a result of vandalism.

think about…

Why do young people get involved in vandalism?
- What should be done with a young person caught vandalising public property?
- What would you do if you saw someone spraying graffiti on a fence or garage door?
- In what ways can vandalism be dangerous?

TAKING ACTION IN SOCIETY
Here are some of the ways people might get involved in their community, especially if they feel strongly about something:
- Voting
- Getting involved in politics
- Joining a pressure group
- Signing a petition
- Protesting against an issue
- Writing a letter to a MP or newspaper
- Taking part in voluntary work
- Supporting a charity
- Taking part in a local 'clean-up' scheme

Can you think of any others?

activity…

WALKING DEBATE
Think about the ways of taking action. Are there any you do now? Would you take part in any of them when you are older?

You could discuss these questions with a partner, or your teacher may organise a walking debate. Different corners of the room will be labelled as shown below. When your teacher calls out something from the list you walk to the appropriate part of the room.

NEVER	LONG TERM FUTURE
SHORT TERM FUTURE	NOW

71

EMPLOYABILITY

WORK IN THE LOCAL AND GLOBAL COMMUNITY

CAREER MANAGEMENT

ENTERPRISE AND ENTREPRENEURSHIP

EMPLOYABILITY

WORK IN THE LOCAL AND GLOBAL COMMUNITY

1. WORK IN NORTHERN IRELAND

We are learning about:
- Some of the different occupations people do
- How people's occupations are changing
- Job opportunities in your local area

WHAT IS 'EMPLOYABILITY'?

Today, there are many different jobs and career opportunities. By the time you finish your education and are ready to enter the world of work, there will probably be an even greater choice. Our daily lives are becoming more complex and technology is playing a greater part in daily living. This is reflected in the jobs that people do. Many people nowadays do not want to do a 'job' just for the money. They want to do something they are interested in and have a career that is rewarding.

"When I grow up, I want to be"

This is why it is important to start thinking ahead to your future career. This does not mean you should already know what you want to do. Employability is all about helping you develop your skills and abilities. You will also discover what qualities you need for different careers. Getting prepared for the world of work is now an important part of what you will learn in school. It is all part of your career plan, which has already started and Year 8 will be an important time for you!

For discussion…
- Can you remember how old you were when you first had some ideas about your future career?
- What job did you want to do?
- Do you still want to do this work, or looking back was it not a practical idea?
- Do you have any career ideas now?
- Discuss your ideas with others in the class.

MI — TPD — WO — COM

WORK IN NORTHERN IRELAND
The past

Traditionally, many people did farming work. They may have grown crops or raised animals for milk, meat and eggs. Some people had jobs milling grain or weaving cloth. During the nineteenth century, Northern Ireland became famous for manufacturing, particularly linen and shipbuilding. Thousands of people were employed in these areas. Shipbuilding and farming continued to be very important during the Second World War. In the 1960s there were new investments in Northern Ireland and many people were employed in factories making clothes. However, during 'the troubles' some companies were unwilling to come to Northern Ireland and unemployment became a serious concern.

SM — WO — MI — COM   activity…

Interview a family member or friend who is an older person, perhaps someone who has retired.

- Find out how old they were when they started working and what their first job was.
- Did they have this job for all of their working life? Have they had a career change or period of unemployment?
- Do many people today still do this work?
- Share your findings with the rest of the class.

WORK IN THE LOCAL AND GLOBAL COMMUNITY

The present

Farming and manufacturing continue to be important areas of employment. However, there are a number of new areas were people now work today. Here are some examples:

Tourism – Many people are now choosing Northern Ireland as a holiday destination. The top tourist destinations include the Causeway coast and the Glens of Antrim, the Mournes, the Walled City of Derry and the Titanic Museum. An increase in tourism has led to new jobs in hotels and restaurants.

Retail – Large stores and supermarkets provide a variety of occupations. These can include store manager, checkout operator, driver, personal shopper, butcher and even optician! Over the last ten years or so, a number of new businesses have come to Northern Ireland. Many large shops have opened stores, including Tesco, ASDA, Sainsburys and Iceland.

Information Technology – Computers play an important part in our lives and there has been significant growth in this area of employment. Some of the job opportunities include designing websites, developing software and installing computer systems.

Leisure – People like to enjoy their free time. Nowadays, many people have more time and money for leisure activities than their parents or grandparents did. Careers in leisure include those in sport, fitness and entertainment.

Social care – People live longer than they did in the past, as medicine and health care have improved. This means there is an increasing number of older people who need care. A career in Social Care could involve working with children or older people. Nurseries and play groups are increasing in number as many parents choose to go out to work. Care homes for the elderly also provide work for many people.

OUR LOCAL AREA

In the area where you live there will be opportunities for work. These opportunities may differ depending on whether the area is in the countryside or a town. However, in most areas where people live, there will be businesses and services to help them with their daily lives. These might include shops, a post office, a school and a health centre. All of these will provide different opportunities for employment.

Where do people work?

- Supermarket
- Health Centre
- Post Office
- Council Office
- Leisure Centre
- Hospital
- School
- Public Transport
- Hotel
- Restaurant
- Cinema
- Factory
- Shopping Centre
- Hairdressers
- Animal Shelter
- Dentist's Surgery

Are any of these in your local area? What jobs do people do?

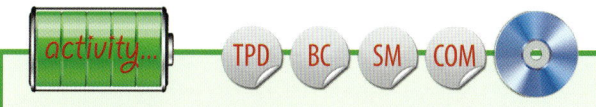

activity...

Work in groups of three or four for this activity.

- Choose a local area. This could be the town or village where you live, or the area around your school.
- In your group, write down the places in the area where people work. Use the suggestions in the box above to help you.
- Each person in the group chooses one place. What are the job opportunities in the workplace you have chosen? Try to think of at least three.
- Use a large piece of card or paper to make a group poster 'Work in our local area'.
- Present your ideas to the rest of the class.

For discussion...

- Do you think there is a good range of employment in the area you have chosen?
- Do you think there is enough work in the area for the people who live there?
- Do some people have to travel to find work?
- Are there any new businesses and services? If so, what jobs do they provide?

EMPLOYABILITY

2. BUYING AND SELLING WORLDWIDE

We are learning about:
- The importance of global trading
- Supporting local traders
- The advantages of the Internet for businesses

BUYING FROM OVERSEAS

Think of all the things you might wear, eat or drink in a day. It is likely that many of these will have been produced in Northern Ireland, perhaps your bottled drink or bread for your lunch. However, if you look at the labels on your clothes or trainers you will see that many of these have come from countries overseas. Many of the electronic items you use, such as your phone, computer or games console, will not have been made in Northern Ireland.

Buying from overseas gives us a greater variety of goods. There are many things that cannot be produced locally, perhaps because of climate. Oranges and bananas need to be imported from countries with sunnier climates. Cost is another consideration as people want to buy goods at the best price. In some parts of the world, people are prepared to work for lower wages, so items can be sold more cheaply than those made locally.

activity... MI WO TPD

Make two lists.
- In one list, write down the items you use that have been made locally.
- In the other list, write down the items you use that come from overseas.
- If you are not sure about where an item comes from, note it down below your lists and ask the advice of the person sitting beside you.
- What do your lists show about the importance of buying and selling worldwide?

For discussion…
What would you miss most if you could only buy things that were made in Northern Ireland?

SUPPORTING OUR LOCAL ECONOMY

Many people think it is important to support local farmers by buying things that have been produced in Northern Ireland. Local farm shops selling home grown vegetables and meat are becoming popular. Many of the large supermarkets make a point of selling fresh food that has been produced in Northern Ireland.

For discussion…
What are the advantages of buying local produce?

CASE STUDY: LIDL SUPERMARKETS
Sourced Locally

We work closely with local suppliers to bring you a wealth of products. We take pride in providing you with the best local produce.

- 100% of our Strathvale beef is locally sourced.
- 100% of our Bally Manor chicken is locally sourced.
- 100% of our fresh milk is locally sourced.
- 100% of our eggs are laid and packed in Northern Ireland.

Freshness Guaranteed
We pay particular attention to local, seasonal produce, so you can always find local products at the peak of freshness and flavour for you to enjoy. We are proud to deliver fresh local produce daily.

Information taken from: http://www.lidl-ni.co.uk/cps/rde/xchg/lidl_ni_ie/hs.xsl/13071.htm

WORK IN THE LOCAL AND GLOBAL COMMUNITY

activity... SM MI ICT

What other shops in Northern Ireland try to sell local produce? Use the Internet or have a look at some of the packets in your fridge or cupboard.

IMPORTS AND EXPORTS

Imports are the products which are brought into a country. A country's **exports** are the goods and produce which are sold abroad. Look at the items below.

- cars
- bread
- cocoa
- jeans
- grapes
- medication
- dairy products

Which are imported into Northern Ireland and which ones are our exports?

What other items do we import or export?

Using the Internet
There are many ways a business can benefit from using the Internet:

- **Customers overseas can be reached** – Small businesses on a small budget can reach customers from all over the world. Websites such as eBay and Amazon have helped with this.

- **A wide range of services can be offered** – As well as doing your shopping, you can book a holiday or join a gym online.
The possibilities are endless!

- **Buying and selling can take place 24/7** – The Internet is immediate and you do not have to worry about opening hours. Goods can be bought and tickets booked at any time.

activity... WO MI TPD

Read the following examples and discuss the questions with a partner.

1. Could using the Internet help these small businesses to be more successful?
2. Do you think their business would be suitable for local people or customers further away?

- *Linda* is a registered child minder. She looks after pre-school age children in her own home during the day.
- *Alan* lives in the country. He has his own chickens, grows organic vegetables and also keeps bees. A local shop sells his eggs, honey and vegetables.
- *Electronic Solutions* is a small company selling circuit boards and parts for computers. They do a lot of mail order business.
- *Siobhan* runs Snipz, a hairdressing salon. She wants to expand her business and do fake tans and gel nails as well as hair.
- *Tony* is a silversmith, specialising in handmade silver jewellery. He sells the items he makes in his small shop.

EMPLOYABILITY

3. NEW TECHNOLOGY

We are learning about:
- Technology in daily life
- The use of technology in schools
- The impact of technology in the workplace

For discussion…
Are there any other new technologies that your school uses?
In what ways do they make school life better for everyone?

TECHNOLOGY IN DAILY LIFE

Can you imagine what your life would be like with no mobile phone, computer, Internet, games condole, or even no television? Your grandparents, and possibly your parents, might remember what it was like not to have some of them. However, for most people today, these things are an essential part of daily life. New technology has an impact on everyone, whether you are keeping in touch with friends, doing your school work or just relaxing at home.

NEWS ITEM

SCHOOLS MUST EMBRACE MOBILE TECHNOLOGY

Schools must embrace mobile technologies, games, podcasts and social networking, according to leading educationalist Professor Stephen Heppell.

At Lampton Secondary School in Hounslow, play is a significant part of the school ethos and children were at the conference demonstrating how games consoles such as the Wii and GPS devices can be integrated into the classroom. Meanwhile at Cleveland Junior School in Redbridge, Year 6 pupils have been busy designing their own computer games. "We made a storyline and introduced characters and designed the backgrounds," explained 11-year-old Rezwana. "More schools should use the software because you can put your own personal thoughts into the game," added classmate Pawan, also aged 11. The games the children made were sent to a nearby infant school where Year 2 pupils played them and suggested improvements via Skype.

But not all schools are so keen to embrace technology. Many still ban the use of mobile phones and social networking sites such as Facebook. "Turned off devices equals turned off children. Sensible schools use mobile technology to their advantage, putting up a telephone number about an issue such as bullying and getting pupils to text their views," said Prof Heppell.

'Schools must embrace mobile technology', BBC NEWS, 14 January 2010, accessed 11 December 2012, http://news.bbc.co.uk/1/hi/technology/8457679.s

TECHNOLOGY IN SCHOOL

New technology is being used more and more in education, to improve your learning and make the running of the school more efficient. Which of the following do you have in your school?

- Interactive whiteboards in classrooms
- ipads and tablets instead of notebooks
- E-books instead of textbooks
- Biometric registration, where you can be marked present in school by using a fingerprint reader
- A cashless canteen or cafeteria, where you use a swipe card (or your fingerprint) to buy your lunch

WORK IN THE LOCAL AND GLOBAL COMMUNITY

For discussion…
Do you agree or disagree with the opinions in the news item?

You could organise a class debate with the motion:

'This house believes that schools should use mobile technology, games and social networking in lessons.'

activity… WO MI TPD COM

Work in groups of about three or four.
- On a large sheet of paper, create a spider diagram of the different technologies you use everyday, at home or at school.
- Talk about the effect these have on your daily life. Could you manage without them?
- Share your ideas with the rest of the class.

TECHNOLOGY IN THE WORKPLACE

New technology is also being used in the workplace. Many of the traditional ways of doing things are changing as a result. You have probably noticed that shopping has changed. Your parents or carers might not go to the supermarket but order the weekly groceries online and get them delivered. In agriculture, farmers are using satellites to decide which part of their land is best suited to certain crops, or what fertilisers a particular field needs. People expect a hotel to have fast broadband speeds and a number of remote controlled gadgets in the room.

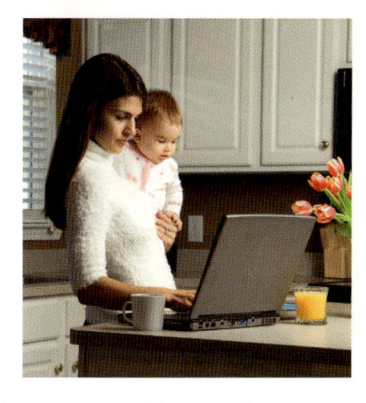

Technology has changed the workplace a lot in the last few years. It has given advances in equipment, new ways of communication and greater efficiency. It can include keypads for workers to get into a secured area, security monitors and cameras, computers, fax machines, photocopiers and telephone systems. Most people now have a computer and a telephone inside their home and thousands of people can work from home instead of commuting to the office. This can save money for both the worker and employer. The employee also saves money on transport costs and possibly childcare. It might be possible to work from home and look after young children at the same time.

Employees with a disability
New computer technology is being developed for the workplace to help employees who are disabled. This is called assistive technology. May jobs now need IT skills, but for some disabled people, standard equipment can be difficult for them to use. Special screen reading software has been developed so people who are blind can use computers. Words on the screen are converted into speech. Braille readouts can also be produced on a special display under the keyboard. A person with a physical disability may find it difficult to use a standard key board or mouse. There are alternatives available, which include one-handed key boards and screen pointers which can be controlled with almost any part of the body.

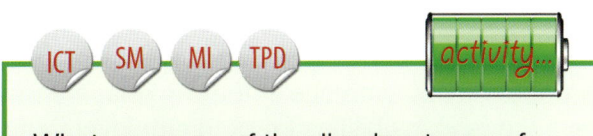

ICT SM MI TPD activity…

What are some of the disadvantages of new technology in the workplace?

Use the Internet to find out some of the challenges for local businesses.

EMPLOYABILITY

4. HEALTH AND SAFETY

We are learning about:
- The importance of taking responsibility for your own health and safety
- Health and safety in the workplace
- The responsibilities of employers and employees

IT'S EVERYONE'S RESPONSIBILITY!

Whether you are at home, in school or out and about, you need to take some responsibility for your health and safety. Parents, carers and teachers have a duty to make sure you are safe. However, it is your responsibility to make sure you follow any rules or guidelines given to you for your safety.

It is the same in the world of work. Employers have a responsibility to make sure their employees are protected from hazards and dangers in the workplace. Workers must make sure they follow health and safety rules and wear the correct clothing or equipment to protect them. Health and safety is important. If one person is acting in an irresponsible way, it not only puts themselves at risk but others as well.

HEALTH AND SAFETY IN THE WORKPLACE

Health and safety is all about reducing the risk of an injury or preventing people from becoming ill through their work. Health and safety is the responsibility of everyone in the workplace and there are responsibilities for both employers and employees.

Responsibilities for the employer

The employer has to make sure that health and safety laws are kept. There are laws in place to make sure that workplaces are safe. The **Health and Safety Executive for Northern Ireland** is responsible for making sure these regulations are carried out and it can inspect places of work. Employers also must carry out a **risk assessment**. This means they have to decide what could cause harm to someone in the workplace. They then have to take steps to control these risks. For example, a noisy piece of machinery might cause damage to hearing. The employer could make a rule for the workplace that all employees using this machinery must wear the special ear protection which is provided. A risk assessment is important as it helps an employer focus on the health and safety issues in their workplace.

An employer has to make sure that staff are trained properly in health and safety so they can keep themselves safe at work. Everyone should know where to go to receive first aid and what to do in an emergency. Health and safety information might be displayed in the workplace as a poster on a notice board. New staff might be given a presentation about health and safety when they start work.

Responsibilities for the employee

All employees have responsibility for health and safety. These include:
- taking care with their own health and safety and using any safety equipment that is provided.
- taking care not to put anyone else at risk through their behaviour.
- cooperating with their employers and following the health and safety policies for their workplace.

WORK IN THE LOCAL AND GLOBAL COMMUNITY

WHAT ARE THE HAZARDS?

You might think that the modern workplace is a safe place to be, with so many rules and regulations. However, this is often not the case! Many people get serious illnesses or are badly hurt at work because either they or their employers do not put health and safety first:

- **Slips and trips** – Wet or greasy floors, or a spill that no-one has the time to mop up, can be the cause of many accidents in the workplace.
- **Falls** – Falling from a height such as a ladder, roof or piece of machinery can be a common cause of injury.
- **Asthma** – What do a school cook, a woodworker and a lab assistant working with animals all have in common? They can all be at risk from developing asthma as they work with materials that produce dust, such as sawdust, flour and animal bedding.
- **Noise** – Constantly listening to loud noises can cause damage to hearing. This can be a problem for factory workers, the runway crew at an airport or even bar staff in a nightclub.
- **Stress** – Workplace stress is a growing problem that is causing people to become ill. There are many causes of stress at work such as bullying, not getting on with other workers or not being properly trained to do a job.

Can you think of any other ways that people might be made unwell or get hurt through their work?

activity... WO TPD MI ICT

Work with a partner. For each of the situations above, think of ways for an employer to cut down on the risk of accident and injury to workers. You could use the Internet to help you.

Remember

Although all this might seem a long way off at the moment, in a couple of years' time you will be old enough to start part time work. Whether you are doing a paper round, babysitting or working in a local shop for a few hours, you will need to think about keeping yourself safe at work.

CASE STUDY: TAYTO CRISPS

The popular crisps are made at the factory at Tayto Castle in Tandragee. Tayto make sure that the highest standards of safety and hygiene are followed by the members of staff who work on the factory floor, handling the potatoes, crisps and snacks.

- Hair must be tucked into a disposable cap
- A white coat must be worn
- No make up, nail polish or jewellery can be worn
- No mobile phones on the factory floor
- Safety Shoes must be worn by all staff
- Pockets must be empty
- No eating or drinking on the factory floor

These regulations are displayed on notice boards throughout the factory.

activity... SM MI TPD

In the workplace, symbols are often used to show dangers and hazards. These symbols are easy to recognise. You may have seen some of them around your school. See how many you recognise.

81

EMPLOYABILITY

CAREER MANAGEMENT

5. WHAT AM I GOOD AT?

We are learning about:
- Career planning
- Your personal qualities and skills
- Key skills for learning and employment

STARTING POINT

Right now, you may not have any idea about the job you want. In fact, you probably have a better idea of what you don't want to spend the rest of your life doing! Thinking about what you are good at and why can be a starting point for career plans. If your future job uses your skills and is something that interests you, then you are more likely to find the work rewarding and enjoyable. Using a mind map can be a good way to help you make connections between your interests, skills and abilities.

YOUR PERSONAL QUALITIES

Most people have a mixture of strengths and weaknesses. Knowing what your personal skills and qualities are can help you to choose a career that is right for you. Everyone has skills. Being skilled doesn't just mean that you always come top in exams, or that you are the best hockey player in your year. There are many different skills in life. Knowing what you are naturally good at can help when you are thinking about future careers.

SIMON: "I love doing things. I am best at the subjects where we do practicals, like science, technology and home economics."

JENNY: "I have a good memory and find it easy to learn my work. My Spanish teacher says I am getting on well with learning a new language. I also enjoy maths but I am useless at sport!"

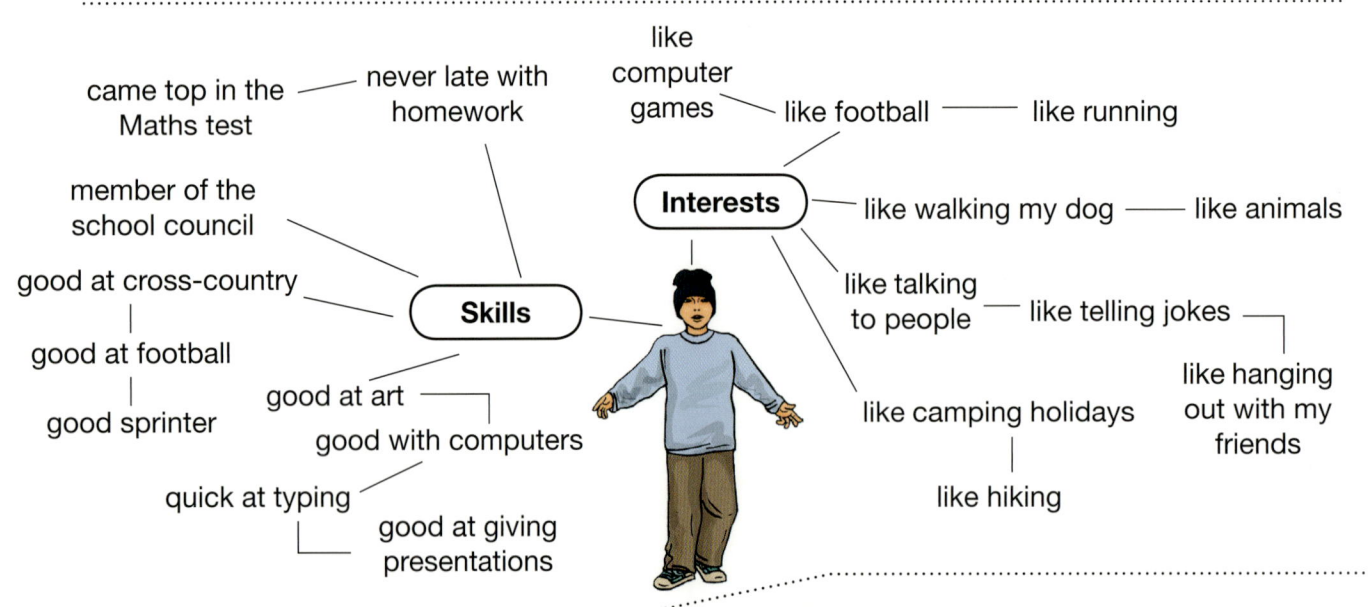

Skills:
- came top in the Maths test
- never late with homework
- member of the school council
- good at cross-country
- good at football
- good sprinter
- good at art
- good with computers
- quick at typing
- good at giving presentations

Interests:
- like computer games
- like football
- like running
- like walking my dog
- like animals
- like talking to people
- like telling jokes
- like camping holidays
- like hanging out with my friends
- like hiking

activity — BC MI TPD
Create your own mind map to show your interests and experiences, skills and abilities.

activity — SM MI TPD
Look at the qualities at the top of the next page and decide which ones belong to you. Make a list beginning with the words "**I am…**"

CAREER MANAGEMENT

sincere tolerant responsible artistic
imaginative
adventurous reliable
forgetful determined loyal
polite humorous shy
generous caring assertive out-going
easy-going patient flexible enthusiastic
creative calm trustworthy honest passive
dependable punctual hard working sympathetic tactful
independent courageous self-confident

Using the words in your list, write a few sentences about your character and personality. What type of career might be suitable for someone with your qualities?

KEY SKILLS

Key skills are the basic skills that affect everything you do in school. They will continue to be important when you leave education and enter the world of work. You will probably find that you are naturally better at some key skills than others. However, it is important to develop your skills in all the key areas. There is a lot you can do to help yourself with the ones you are not so good at.

activity... SM MI TPD

See how many key skills you already have and which ones you need to develop.

Communication skills
- Can you speak clearly and give a short talk or presentation?
- Are you good at different types of writing, such as producing a report or a letter?
- When you take part in discussions, do you listen to the views of others?
- Can you read and understand different types of writing?

Numeracy skills
- Can you carry out calculations?
- Do you find it easy to understand information given in tables and graphs?
- Can you present and explain what you have found out?
- Can you measure accurately?

ICT skills
- Can you use a computer to solve problems?
- Are your word processing skills improving?
- Can you use a computer to find and store information?
- Do you know how to use a spreadsheet?

Study skills
- Are you good at organising your notes and homework?
- Can you carry out research and produce projects?
- Can you review your progress and improve your own learning?
- Do you revise for tests effectively?

Problem-solving skills
- Do you ask questions and make observations?
- Can you give suggestions and offer solutions to problems?
- Do you check to see if your solutions have worked?
- Are you good at forming an opinion and making a conclusion?

Personal and social skills
- Are you good at getting on with others?
- Have you settled into your new school and made friends?
- Do you listen to and understand other people's points of view?
- Can you work with other people as part of a team?

activity... TPD MI

Write down "**I can…**" statements to show skills that you have in your daily life. Try to match each one to a key skill. For example:

- **I can…** Use the Internet to find out what time a film starts at the cinema and email my friend. **Key skill:** ICT

- **I can…** Look at my school report and plan how to improve my grades. **Key skill:** Study skills

EMPLOYABILITY

6. THINKING ABOUT MY CAREER

We are learning about:
- Why people work
- Targets and goals
- The need for personal planning

WHY DO PEOPLE WORK?
There many reasons why people work. Here are some suggestions:

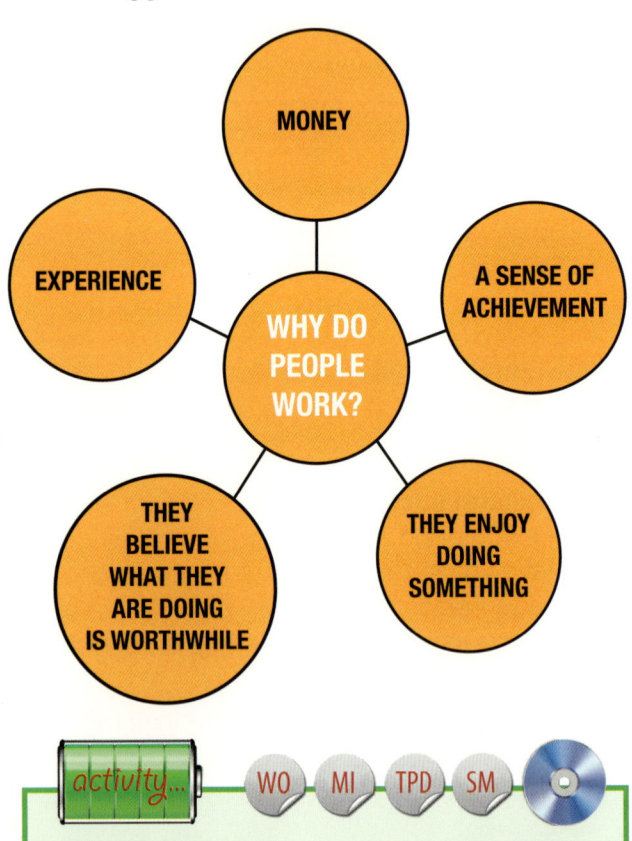

Spider diagram: WHY DO PEOPLE WORK? — MONEY, A SENSE OF ACHIEVEMENT, THEY ENJOY DOING SOMETHING, THEY BELIEVE WHAT THEY ARE DOING IS WORTHWHILE, EXPERIENCE

activity... WO | MI | TPD | SM

Can you think of any other reasons? Draw a spider diagram of your own. What do you think are the most important reasons for doing a job? Share your ideas with a partner.

SETTING TARGETS AND REACHING GOALS
In the last section, we looked at the importance of key skills in school and for the workplace. Managing your work effectively in school can be an important step towards managing your future career. Part of this process is to set targets for yourself and work towards goals.

What do we mean by targets and goals?
In sports, a goal is a hoop, area or cage and the objective of many team games is to get the ball into it. A target, used in shooting or archery, is something to aim at. Whatever stage of life someone is at, whether a school pupil, an employee or a retired person, it is important to have a goal to aim for. This could be doing well in your Year 8 exams, getting an important promotion or taking up a new hobby. To be successful, you need to take steps to get there. Your targets are the steps you take towards achieving your goal.

What is a SMART goal?
The letters of the word SMART are sometimes used to describe successful goals.

S — **Specific:** Your goal should be clear and straightforward.

M — **Measurable:** You know how far away your goal is and when it has been reached.

A — **Attainable:** Your goal needs to be a challenge, but not impossible.

R — **Realistic:** You need to consider your abilities when setting your goal.

T — **Time based:** You should have a time limit that your targets help you get to.

CAREER MANAGEMENT

CASE STUDY: LORRAINE

Lorraine is in Year 8. She has just received her school report for the end of her first term and is very disappointed. Lorraine thinks she has settled in well, likes her new school and has made friends. However, many of her teachers think she is too disorganised and often misses homework deadlines. Science has always been Lorraine's favourite subject but she did very badly in a recent class test. She left her revision until the last minute then realised she did not understand one of the topics.

Lorraine's goal
To get a better report at the end of the year, especially for science.

Lorraine's targets:
1. To record all the work teachers set in her homework diary.
2. To complete all her homework before watching television.
3. To organise all her notes and copy up anything that is missing.
4. To ask her science teacher to explain the work she does not understand.
5. To start revising early for the end of year tests.

How well do you organise your work?

It is important to have good study habits. Having an organised approach to your work will help you improve in your subjects and help you to develop your key skills.

---

activity...

Decide on a personal goal for yourself.

Work out what targets you need to aim for in order to reach your goal.

What things might stop you from reaching your goal? Try to set targets that will help to avoid this.

---

activity...

Answer the following questions honestly and see how many you can answer YES to. The more YESes, the better your study habits are.

1. Do you usually get your work in on time?
2. Do you keep a record of work that is set in a homework diary?
3. Do you set aside a regular time for doing your school work each evening?
4. Do you always know where to find your notes and books?
5. Before starting work, do you decide what the most urgent task is and do this first?
6. Do you turn off your phone and make sure you are not distracted while studying?
7. Do you take regular breaks when you are studying to keep up your concentration levels?
8. Do you highlight key points or make revision notes when you have to learn something?

EMPLOYABILITY

7. INVESTIGATING JOBS

We are learning about:
- The importance of fulfilling work
- Skills and qualities needed for certain jobs
- Some of the possible career options available

DOING SOMETHING YOU ENJOY

Some people know from an early age what they want to do in life. They make this their ambition and go on to achieve their goal. Some people are very talented in a particular area, such as sport, music or drama and are lucky enough to make this their career. Earning a living from something that most people enjoy as a leisure activity is very difficult. If you plan to be a professional musician or athlete, it would be best to have a back-up plan.

Sometimes a person can end up in their chosen career by accident, or very late on. Perhaps they started out in one career and then decided it was not for them. A person with skills and qualifications, or the willingness to do more training is in a better position to change direction in their career.

SKILLS AND QUALITIES

Knowing what your interests are and what you enjoy doing is important when considering careers. You also need to think about what skills and qualities are needed for a particular job and whether it could be the right one for you.

activity...   MI TPD SM

For each of the following occupations, list the skills ('**I can…**') and the personal qualities ('**I am…**') that the person needs for this career.

- Thomas is a **care assistant** in a residential home for the elderly.

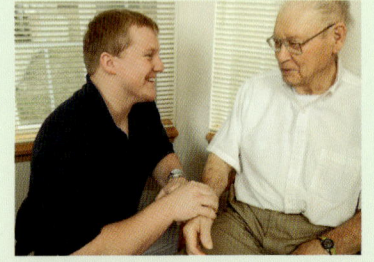

- Anna is a **beautician** who runs her own business.

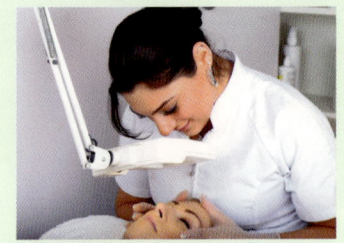

- Daragh is **manager of a leisure centre.**

- Amanda is an **estate agent,** helping people to buy and sell their own homes.

FOCUS ON CAREERS
Do you like reading?

There are plenty of career possibilities for bookworms. A job as a librarian might suit you, where you could share your love of reading and knowledge of books with others. Perhaps you could volunteer to help out in your school library to see if you like library work. If you also like writing you might want to work as an editorial journalist for a newspaper or magazine, a copywriter for an advertising firm or as an editor for a book publisher. You might prefer a career in research, which could involve a lot of reading and if you like languages, you might think about becoming a translator.

CAREER MANAGEMENT

Are you good at sport?

It is difficult to make a living in professional sport, and only a few lucky people make it to the top. However, there are a large number of jobs available in the sports and leisure because fitness is a growing industry and people are spending more and more time on leisure activities. Careers in sport include working in a leisure centre, becoming a PE teacher, sports coach, personal trainer, physiotherapist or outdoor pursuits instructor. If you are interested in sport there are also opportunities for a career in the media, perhaps as a sports journalist.

Are you interested in fashion?

If you like fashion and keeping up with the latest trends, then a career in the fashion industry might be for you. The term 'fashion industry' involves anyone involved in the designing, making, promoting and selling of clothes to the public. Becoming a model might seem an obvious career choice, but remember that only a lucky few get to make a full time living from modelling. If you are creative, then fashion design might suit you. There are also a wide variety of careers in the retail industry, including sales assistant and store manager. Fashion buying involves choosing the clothes for a shop to sell, trying to get value for money and something that will sell well.

Would you enjoy working with animals?

If you love animals and they really seem to take to you, then you might think about a career that involves working with them. One option is to go to university and train to be a vet, although you would need to be very good at science and maths, and committed to many years of hard study. Other options include working in a veterinary practice, either as a veterinary nurse or an animal care assistant, an animal shelter, boarding kennels or a zoo. These careers all involve feeding, helping and caring for the animals. There are also careers in marine and wildlife biology, dog training and walking, livestock farming, and horse grooming and riding.

Would you like to do something worthwhile?

For many people, there is more to a satisfying career that a large salary. Some people get job satisfaction from helping others or doing something valuable in the local community. You might think about working for a charity or voluntary organisation, perhaps as a fundraiser or publicity officer. The salary may not be large, but the job satisfaction could make up for this. You might prefer a career in medicine and train to be a nurse, care assistant, doctor or a paramedic. Or maybe social work or counselling is for you, where you can help people with their problems. You might even consider becoming a firefighter. Although the work can be dangerous and dirty, you might get a lot of satisfaction from helping the community.

---

activity...   SM   MI   TPD

It can be difficult to decide what you want to be when there are so many choices. You might find it helpful to think about what kind or person you are and what you would love or hate to do. Try the quiz on the CD to find out what you are good at.

EMPLOYABILITY

ENTERPRISE AND ENTREPRENEURSHIP

8. ARE YOU AN ENTERPRISING PERSON?

We are learning about:
- The qualities of enterprising people
- Examples of people who are enterprising
- What is an entrepreneur?

WHAT DO WE MEAN BY 'ENTERPRISING'?

Some people can be described as 'enterprising'. No two people are exactly alike, but enterprising people usually share some of these characteristics:

- They are motivated and determined to achieve.
- They believe they have the qualities to be successful.
- They are creative, often setting up new projects or looking for new opportunities.
- They are willing to take risks rather than 'play safe'.
- They show determination and keep going even when things do not go well.

To sum up, enterprising people make things happen and they make a difference in both their own lives and the lives of others.

think about...

SM / TPD — People who lack enterprise may miss out on exciting new opportunities. Do you think you need to be more enterprising? How could you do this?

Ten qualities of an enterprising person

These are some of the words that can be used to describe a person who is enterprising:

1. **Self-motivated** – They give themselves goals and work to achieve them.
2. **Creative** – They come up with new ideas.
3. **Self-confident** – They believe they can do well if they try.
4. **Determined** – They keep going even if things do not go well.
5. **Persistent** – They stick at things and do not give up easily.
6. **Decisive** – They can make a decision and stick to it.
7. **Flexible** – They are not set in a routine.
8. **Competitive** – They want to do better than their rivals.
9. **Enthusiastic** – They really believe in what they are doing.
10. **A leader** – They can inspire others and pass on their enthusiasm.

- Which of these apply to you?
- Can you think of any examples of how you show these qualities in your daily life?
- Could you be described as enterprising?

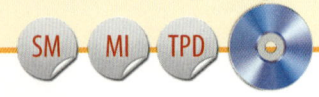

SM — MI — TPD

ENTERPRISING PEOPLE

What people do you know who could be described as enterprising? An enterprising person might be someone from your class or a member of your family; a famous sports personality or a musician; maybe a politician or someone who works hard to help others. The possibilities are endless, as enterprising people come from all walks of life.

Enterprising people show their qualities in different ways. Some people show enterprise in the local community, using their determination to help others rather than making a profit for themselves. Some enterprising people choose personal goals. They might achieve an Olympic gold medal, climb the world's highest mountains, or simply take up a new hobby. For some people, going into business is the ideal way for them to make the most of their enterprising qualities.

The government can show enterprise in the decisions it makes. A few years ago, the car scrappage scheme was introduced. Money was given to a car owner who scrapped a car that was ten years of age or older in order to buy a new car. There were benefits to the environment as older cars can cause more pollution. Road safety also improved as there were less 'old bangers' on the road. The sales for new cars increased, generating money for car dealerships and new jobs were also created.

Many local councils in Northern Ireland are introducing special bins to encourage more recycling rather than sending waste to landfill sites. The following items can be placed in different coloured bins for recycling: paper, food waste, garden waste, plastic bottles and metal cans. These bins are an enterprising solution to the problem of household waste.

activity...

Consider the following examples. In what way can each of these people be described as enterprising?

- **JK Rowling** – The author who created the Harry Potter books, which have become the best selling book series in history.
- **Bob Geldof** – A successful Irish musician who started the charity Band Aid and the Live 8 concerts to help starving people in Africa.
- **Jamie Oliver** – A TV chef. One of his well-known campaigns was about the poor quality of school meals and led to the successful TV series 'Jamie's school dinners'.
- **Victoria Beckham** – A famous pop singer who is now a fashion designer and businesswoman, with her own range of perfume and sunglasses.
- **Clare Francis** – The first woman to sail around the world single-handedly, as well as being a popular author.

WHAT IS AN ENTREPRENEUR?

If a person with enterprising qualities decides to go into business, then the result is likely to be an **'entrepreneur'**. This word is French in origin.

An entrepreneur has an idea and sees an opportunity which other people have not recognised. They take the initiative in setting up a business. They believe they can make this idea a success and are willing to take responsibility for any risks involved. What are the rewards for the clever idea and the risk-taking? Making a profit is a big bonus, but so is the satisfaction of knowing you have achieved something that other people haven't!

activity...

Work in groups of four or five for this activity.

- Your group will be given cards. Place the cards face down and take one each.
- Read about the person on your card.
- Take it in turns to introduce this person to the others in your group. You have to explain to them in what way your character is enterprising.
- Continue until all the cards have been used.
- The group then vote for which person has presented their characters the most effectively.

EMPLOYABILITY

9. HAVING A GOOD IDEA

We are learning about:
- The importance of creativity
- How to get the support of other people
- People who have had good ideas

CLEVER THINKING

Enterprising people are creative. They are often the one to have a good idea or come up with a solution to a problem. Successful entrepreneurs are often the people who have a brainwave or spot a gap in the market for something.

think about...   SM MI TPD

Have you ever had a good idea or clever solution to a problem that no-one else has thought of?

Were you able to carry out your idea?

Was it a success?

It is important to remember that your good idea may not work out. This is why enterprising people are also determined and persistent. They keep trying their idea and do not give up at the first obstacle. However, enterprising people are also flexible. They can make changes to their original idea and have another go at it.

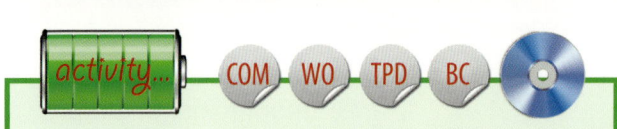

activity...   COM WO TPD BC

ROLE PLAY

In each of the situations below, a young person has had an idea. They are trying to persuade a sceptical friend or family member to agree with them.
Choose a situation to role play and take it in turns to play each character.

1. **The bedroom makeover** – Jill thinks her bedroom is boring and babyish. She has some brilliant plans for a makeover. Jill plans to do the work herself, but has to persuade her mum to pay the bills. Jill's mum is not very keen. How can Jill get her to agree?

2. **Extra pocket money** – Sean's uncle is self-employed. He has a small, successful business doing gardening work for people in the summer and decorating jobs in the winter. Sean wants to earn some money over the summer holidays and has volunteered to help his uncle. One of Sean's ideas is that he will put leaflets through the doors of the houses in their area advertising their services. How can Sean convince his uncle this is a good idea?

3. **A fundraising event** – Megan read an article about the children's hospice in a local magazine. She really wants to do something to raise some much needed cash for this good cause. She has a fundraising idea that her class in school could do. How does Megan persuade her teacher that this would be a really good thing for the class to take part in?

When you are role-playing the young person, remember to be as enterprising as possible. Try to show what good ideas you have and how determined you are!

ENTERPRISE AND ENTREPRENEURSHIP

INVENTIONS, DISCOVERIES AND NEW IDEAS

"How ever did we manage without…"

There are many things in our daily lives that we rely on and we find it hard to imagine life without them. Every day, around the world, computer users spend more than three billion minutes a day on Facebook. Do you share the details of your life by twittering and posting? Millions of people use social networking sites, such as **Facebook, MySpace** and **Twitter** to connect with their friends. Could you survive without your phone? **Text messaging** has become so popular that a whole new vocabulary has been created. LOL and FYI have now passed into everyday use. What other new ideas would you find it hard to be without?

"If at first you don't succeed…"

Sometimes an invention or discovery doesn't work the first time or is slow to catch on. This is why enterprising people need perseverance. Do you wear **trainers**? They have been popular footwear since the 1970s. However, it was in back in 1892 that the Goodyear Metallic Rubber Shoe Company first used a new process to make shoes out of cloth and rubber. At first, no-one liked the new shoes and it took quite a while for the idea to catch on!

Do you use **Post-it notes** to help you remember things or mark the pages of a book? These small sticky sheets of paper first hit the shops in 1981. If it wasn't for a mistake, Post-it notes might not have happened. A researcher called Spencer Silver worked for the 3M Company. He had been trying to invent really powerful glue but his research was a failure. His glue was so weak it was useless.

However, it did peel off any surface easily without leaving a sticky mess. It took another year and a half to get the formula exactly right, but the result was the hugely successful Post-it note.

"Oh dear, time to try again…"

Not all bright ideas end up a success. Failures are all part of the process of invention and help to drive people to greater things. Thomas Edison was one of the greatest inventors ever. He had over 1,000 patents to his name and invented, among other things, light bulbs, movie cameras and Morse code. However, he did have some disastrous failures. One of these was his attempt to make furniture out of 'foam concrete'. He also lost all his money on a scheme to extract metal from iron ore by using magnets.

> **activity…**   ICT   SM   MI
>
> Use the Internet (or books from your school library) to find out about a person who has made a success of a good idea, invention or discovery.
>
> The person you choose might have lived in the past or still be alive today.
>
> Find out about this person's life and work. What led to their success? How are our lives better because of their work?

Finally…

By learning about other people's creative ideas, maybe this will inspire you. Who knows, you might be a successful entrepreneur or inventor of the future!

EMPLOYABILITY

10. GOING INTO BUSINESS

We are learning about:
- The importance of creativity and new ideas
- Designing and marketing a product
- The need for careful planning when setting up in business

Have you ever thought of an original idea for a business or product you think would sell? Perhaps you are creative and can come up with ideas for gadgets and inventions. Or maybe you could spot an opportunity to provide a service no-one else has thought of. With the right marketing, could your idea be a success? Many people dream of running their own business and being their own boss. However, running your own business can be difficult. There are many issues that need to be considered.

THE INGREDIENTS OF A SUCCESSFUL BUSINESS

Behind a successful business there will be an enterprising person or business partners. There will also be some creativity, clever thinking and good ideas. However, even though these are important ingredients, on their own they may not be enough to guarantee success. Careful research and thorough planning are needed before starting out in business. When the product is ready, it will be important to think about how it will be advertised. You need to get your idea noticed and attract as many customers as possible.

BUSINESS SUCCESS

Bill Gates is head of Microsoft. In 1999 he was said to be the richest man on earth. His fortune had been made in less than 20 years. It was based on clever ideas, some risk-taking and making the most of opportunities.

Michael Dell was a 19 year old student in Texas when he started his own PC company. He had the idea that people would prefer to buy a computer directly from the manufacturer, rather than from a shop. Fifteen years later, Dell is one of the largest computer companies in the world.

Geoff Read worked in a shoe shop in London when he realised there could be an opportunity for selling bottled water back home in Ireland. Ballygowan mineral water was the result of his clever thinking.

EMPLOYABILITY PROJECT

Work in groups of four for this activity.

You and the members of your group are business partners. Your task is to design a product, market it and consider how you will run your business.

At the end of the activity, you may be given the opportunity to assess the other groups in your class and decide how successful they have been.

ENTERPRISE AND ENTREPRENEURSHIP

1. Designing your product
In your group, discuss your business idea. You can choose one of the following to design:

- A toy for a child between three and five years of age. The toy should be fun but also educational. It will be able to help a young child with their numbers and letters.
- A piece of equipment for a pet owner. It will help busy people to take the best possible care of their pets. You will need to decide what animal your idea is suitable for.
- A service you can offer in your local area that no-one seems to have thought of. Try to be as creative as you can!

You will need to decide on the design of your product. It is important to have something that will appeal to customers.

Think about the colour, shape and what materials you will use.

- Does your design have to be washable or waterproof?
- How strong does it have to be?
- Is your design safe for use with animals or children?
- If you are offering a service, you will need to think how you can make it appealing to people. Are you going to collect children from school, tidy up gardens or offer a dog walking service?

You will also need to think of a name for your product or service.

Draw and label a picture of your design or the service you intend to offer.

2. Selling your product
Next, you will need to decide how you are going to persuade people to buy your product or use your service:

- What are its important features?
- How will it make people's lives easier or better?
- Where would be the best place to advertise your idea to reach the right people?

Design an advertisement for your product.

3. Setting up in business
Finally, discuss with the others in your group:

- Whether you will need to have any special buildings for your business, or could you operate from someone's home?
- Will your product be on sale in shops or will you sell it on the Internet?
- If you are offering a service, will you need somewhere to operate from or will you go to customers' homes?

Make a list of all the things you need to think about before setting up in business.

You might decide to present your work for this task in the form of a PowerPoint presentation that you can show to the rest of your class.

WO — BC — TPD — MI — COM — ICT

think about... What have you learnt from this activity about the importance of careful planning when starting a business?

YOUNG ENTERPRISE
Young Enterprise Northern Ireland runs programmes that inspire young people from ages 4–25 with the confidence, ability and ambition to succeed. The aim is to inspire entrepreneurship in Northern Ireland. Young Enterprise recognises that the world in which young people live is ever-changing. They continually develop their programmes to make sure young people can get the skills they need to be enterprising and creative.

All Young Enterprise programmes fit in with what young people are learning in school. They benefit our future economy by giving pupils first-hand experience of business. This approach can inspire young people to become the entrepreneurs of the future.

Is there a Young Enterprise scheme in your school? If so, you might be interested in getting involved.

COPYRIGHT INFORMATION

Copyright has been acknowledged to the best of our ability. If there are any inadvertent errors or omissions, we shall be happy to correct them in any future editions.

ACKNOWLEDGEMENTS

Thanks to the following organisations and copyright holders for their kind permission to use their logos, titles, images and information:

> British Red Cross, ChildHope, Lidl, Simon Community, Shelter, Tayto Group Ltd, UNICEF

LICENCES

The following images are licensed under the Creative Commons Attribution 3.0 Unported License. Permission is granted to share and/or remix, and to make commercial use of this work provided the work is attributed in the manner specified by the author or licensor (but not in any way that suggests that they endorse you or your use of the work). A copy of this license can be viewed at http://creativecommons.org/licenses/by/3.0/legalcode

> Page 48 (top right), 65 (left)

The following image is licensed under the Creative Commons Attribution-ShareAlike 2.0 Generic License. Permission is granted to copy, distribute, display, and perform the work, to make derivative works and to make commercial use of the work provided the original author is given credit and if the work is altered, transformed or built upon, the resulting work is distributed only under a license identical to this one. A copy of this license can be viewed at http://creativecommons.org/licenses/by-sa/2.0/legalcode:

> Page 48 (top left)

The following image is licensed under the Creative Commons Attribution 2.0 Generic License. Permission is granted to share and/or remix, and to make commercial use of this work provided the work is attributed in the manner specified by the author or licensor (but not in any way that suggests that they endorse you or your use of the work).

> Page 48 (bottom)

PICTURE CREDITS

All photographs are by iStockphoto except for the following which are included with kind permission of the copyright holders. The numbers denote page numbers.

- Amy (Little Red Pen): 48 top right
- Anthony Upton/British Red Cross: 61 (right)
- David Lobo: 48 (bottom)
- Informatique (William Murphy): 48 (top left)
- Michael McCullough: 2 (author photo)
- Robert Paul Young: 65 (left)
- Tayto Group Ltd: 81
- The International Federation of Red Cross and Red Crescent Societies (IFRC): 60, 61 (left)
- UNICEF: 62

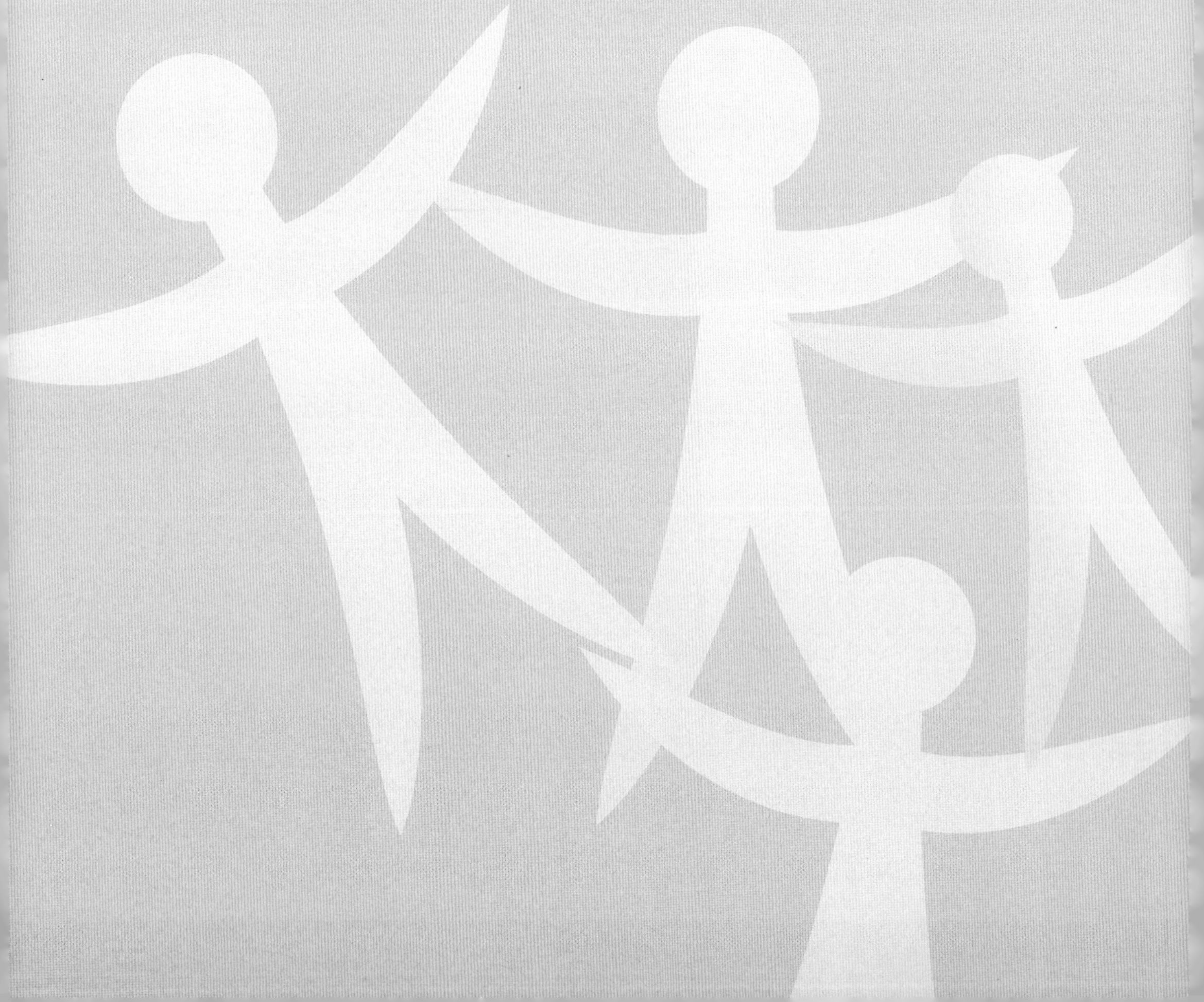